INFLATION
Demand-Pull or Cost-Push?

INFLATION
Demand-Pull or
Cost-Push?

Edited with an introduction by
RICHARD PERLMAN
UNIVERSITY OF WISCONSIN — MILWAUKEE

D. C. HEATH AND COMPANY · BOSTON

COPYRIGHT © 1965, BY D. C. HEATH AND COMPANY
Boston · Englewood · Chicago · Dallas
San Francisco · Atlanta · London · Toronto

No part of the material covered by this copyright may be reproduced in any form without written permission of the publisher. Printed in the United States of America.

Library of Congress Catalog Card Number: 65–18411

PRINTED APRIL 1965

CONTENTS

I. THE CASE FOR DEMAND PULL

II. TWO VIEWS OF THE COST-PUSH ARGUMENT

III. ARE WAGE GUIDEPOSTS THE ANSWER?

IV. INFLATION AND ECONOMIC CHANGE

INTRODUCTION

Perhaps the recent preoccupation of American economists and the general public with the problem of inflation has been caused by the changing pattern of price movements. In the past, inflations were associated with wars and their aftermath. Once the wartime pressures on prices had relaxed, the general levels of prices receded, if not to their previous prewar levels, at least substantially. After World War II, however, or more precisely, after the effects of the removal of wartime price controls had run their course, the historical pattern changed as prices seemed to lose their downward flexibility. The period from 1948 to 1950, which by past experience should have been one of declining prices, was one of relative price stability.

The sharp price increase of the Korean War years was again followed by a period of steady prices until the middle of 1955. Then prices rose for three years until the middle of 1958. Although this price increase was by no means comparable in intensity to the war-associated inflations, this "creeping inflation" of about 2.5 percent per year in general prices was unusual since it occurred in part during a period of business recession. Similar price increases during periods of unemployment had occurred in the mid-1930's, but the inflation of that period was generally attributed to the combined effects of government policy and the recovery from the dismal economic drop and deflation of the 1929–1933 period. There was a similar depression-recovery pattern in prices during our other great depression of the 1870's.

Since about the middle of 1958 prices have shown a remarkable stability. Consumer prices have risen at an annual rate of about 1 per cent per year over the period, which for even the most avid believer in stable prices does not represent an inflationary experience. Wholesale prices have remained practically unchanged since 1958. Therefore at the present writing (1965), the American economy has had seven years of relative price stability. There have been, however, lengthy periods of price stability in the past, the last being 1923–1929.

The table below presents price movements since World War II, separated into periods of inflation and price stability.

CONSUMER PRICE MOVEMENTS SINCE 1945 (INDEX: 1957–1959 = 100)

	INFLATIONS			PRICE STABILITY	
Years		Index	Years		Index
1945	End of World	62.7	1948		83.8
1948	War II price controls	83.8	1950		83.8
	% Increase	33.7%	% Increase		0.0%
	Average Annual % Increase	10.2%	Average Annual % Increase		0.0%
1950	Korean War	83.8	1952		92.5
1952		92.5	1955		93.3
	% Increase	10.7%	% Increase		0.9%
	Average Annual % Increase	5.2%	Average Annual % Increase		0.3%
1955	"Creeping	93.3	1958		100.7
1958	inflation"	100.7	1963		106.3
	% Increase	8.0%	% Increase		5.5%
	Average Annual % Increase	2.6%	Average Annual % Increase		1.1%

Source: Bureau of Labor Statistics. Turning points are more evident for monthly than for annual data. Wholesale prices showed a greater increase than consumer prices during the immediate post-World War II and Korean War inflations and the same rise during the creeping inflation.

In the United States and other advanced economies a rate of price increases of more than 2 per cent annually elicits concern or discussion about the "inflation." For developing countries, a much higher price rise is required before inflation is considered a problem. Among Latin American countries, Mexico, which has experienced an average annual price increase of 7 per cent over the past decade, is often pointed out as a country in which effective monetary policy has prevented substantial price increases.

Economists are in disagreement over both the causes of and remedies for inflation. There is even some question, especially in developing countries, whether inflation is harmful to a country.

Causes of Inflation

In a free enterprise economy the decision to raise prices is made by the businessman who reacts to economic pressures or opportunities by raising the prices of the goods he sells. However, when economists speak of the causes of inflation, they mean the underlying causes of the pressures and opportunities; and only occasionally do they assign prime responsibility to the decision-making business unit itself. Generally speaking, there are two schools of thought on the causes of inflation. These two views have come to be summarized under the headings of *demand-pull* and *cost-push*.

Demand-Pull Inflation

According to the demand-pull theory, prices rise in response to an excess of general demand over existing supply. Adherents to this theory follow the traditional definition of inflation as the result of a situation in which money expenditures exceed output at current prices. The theory receives support when prices rise during a period of full employment, shortages of goods, and production bottlenecks, as occurred after World War II and during the Korean War.

Although demand-pull theorists admit that the pressures on prices are great during a period of excess demand, they look further for the cause of inflation to the reason for the excess demand. The relaxation of pent-up demand and shortages of consumer goods following World War II and accompanying the Korean War might have been the basic source of excess demand, but the parties responsible for making this demand effective and for allowing the consequent inflation were permissive monetary and fiscal authorities. When inflation threatens on the demand side, the monetary authorities can, by strong action affecting interest rates and the supply of money, check the surging demand. In addition, excess demand for goods can be drained off by a fiscal policy which increases tax rates. In neither of the war-associated inflations did the monetary or fiscal authorities act vigorously enough to eliminate the inflationary pressures.

According to the demand-pull hypothesis, pent-up excessive demand, made effective by an accumulation of idle balances during the war which were not offset by deflationary monetary and fiscal policies, pulled prices up. Wage increases that accompanied or followed the price rise were a consequence rather than a cause of the inflation. As producers tried to satisfy the excess demand, they bid against each other for labor or more easily acceded to union wage demands in order to prevent production stoppages during this profitable period.

In this expenditure-price spiral, organized labor's role was a passive and defensive one. Had unions not demanded wage increases during the period, workers would have suffered sharp declines in their real wages as prices rose while money wages remained constant. Yet even without union activity, competition for labor would have bid up wages. The price-setters themselves were the agents and not the prime movers in the inflation, since they merely acted in a manner to clear markets for goods. Had firms not raised their prices, the wartime situation of shortages would have been repeated. Prices would no longer have played their role of equilibrating market supply and demand. For firms to have maintained their prices in the face of excessive demand would have been for them to have acted as if a system of price controls and rationing were still in effect.

The demand-pull inflation could have been averted, after the removal of direct wartime controls, only if the monetary and fiscal authorities had imposed indirect checks on prices through deflationary measures. Although the demand-pull theorists hold passive monetary and fiscal policy responsible for this type of inflation, they see harmful side effects in the steps required to retard inflation. Deflationary steps, with credit restrictions hampering business investment and consumer purchases, and with tax increases reducing purchasing power in general, might depress the economy. The issue here, however, is not whether steps should be taken to stem inflation but what causes inflation. Demand-pull theorists agree that neutral monetary and fiscal policies permit excessive demand to raise prices.

Cost-Push Inflation

An opposite view of the prime cause of inflation holds that the process of inflation is initiated not by an excess of demand but by an increase in costs, as factors of production try to increase their share of the total product by raising their prices. Cost-push analysis assumes monopoly elements either in the product market, if a profit push is responsible for inflation, or in the labor market, if a wage push leads to a cost-price spiral. If the product market were perfectly competitive, a price increase imposed by an industry or firm to gain more profits would result in a total loss of sales to competitors. Similarly, with perfect competition in the labor market, a demand for raises in wages to increase labor's share would result in total loss of employment by the workers involved to other workers or other factors of production.

Cost-push theorists rarely consider autonomous attempts to increase profits an important inflationary element. In the first place, profits are generally a small percentage of the total price, so that a rise in profits would have only a slight impact on prices. What is more important, the attempt to raise profits by raising prices would surely be self-defeating in competitive markets where it is assumed that the current price is set at the optimum profit position. In monopolistic markets where an optimum profit price is perhaps not currently being charged, monopolists hesitate to raise prices in the absence of obvious demand-pull elements. Government and public interest in stable prices and the publicity given to such price increases present too great a risk. Finally, the motivation for a profit push is weak since, at least in corporations, those who make the decision to raise prices are not the direct beneficiaries of the price increase. The initial positive effect of a price rise is an increase of profits disposable to stockholders. Although the stockholders often judge the performance of corporate managers by the size of current profits, corporate policy-makers who try to derive indirect benefits from a rise in profits thus produced, risk the possibility of government intervention or possible loss of market to competitors.

For these reasons, cost push has become synonymous with wage push. Moreover, wage push is equated with union push. It is of no importance that in some instances nonunion wages rise equally with union wages, or that union workers often receive the same wage increase they would actually receive were they unorganized; these are instances of wage increases but are not examples of direct wage-push inflation. Nonunion wages rise because of demand-pull elements; they may even rise because firms pay the high union scale in order to forestall unionization. But most often a demand for wage increases, in the absence of a price rise, initiates from union wage practices.

Union leadership and membership have strong motivations and few inhibitions in seeking wage increases. A wage increase is of direct benefit to the workers who bargain for the increase. Further, the harmful effects on workers of a wage increase are indirect. Wage bargainers often believe that a wage increase may be secured at the expense of profits without an increase in prices. (There is only an academic parallel in noting that business leaders might think that they can increase profits without raising prices, by reducing wages.) Of course, if the union wage-bargainers are correct in their assumption that wages can rise without an increase in profits, then there will be no cost-push inflation. The inflation results to the extent that the wage-bargainers are wrong in their assumption that management will not try to defend its profit position by raising prices. Finally, even if union wage-bargainers believe that prices will rise as a result of the wage increases, they might regard the effect on employment to be negligible. This would be so if they consider the elasticity of demand for labor low or the demand for the product to be inelastic. Even if the employment effects may be serious, some union wage-negotiators have greater concern for the positive income effects on those who retain their jobs than for the negative effects of unemployment for some members.

Many cost-push adherents argue that just as in the case of demand pull, government policy is primarily responsible for inflation. To the degree that unions are employment-conscious, the argument runs, union leaders would not press for wage increases which would lead to unemployment under normal market conditions unless they felt that a government full-employment policy would save labor from the unemployment that would result from union wage gains. Without national bargaining, very few union leaders believe that the government would stand ready to guarantee full employment for the comparatively few workers displaced by the increase in wages gained at the bargaining table. Thus, a national policy to reemploy workers displaced by a general cost-push inflation becomes more than a support for union wage demands; it becomes an independent inflationary force.

In the minds of most theorists, wage-push inflation is usually associated with unemployment. Wage-push adherents, however, do not expect the timing of wage inflation and unemployment to mesh perfectly. Some lag is expected between the beginning of a wage-induced inflation and a rise in unemployment. Consider the "creeping inflation" of 1955–1958, often referred to as cost-(wage-)push inflation. Only the period from late 1957 to mid-1958 could be considered a time of substantial unemployment.

Although the harmful employment effects of a wage rise in a *particular firm* or *industry* are obvious, i.e., the displacement of labor by capital equipment and the loss of part of output to competitors whose prices have not risen, it is less clear that a general rise in wages should seriously affect the level of total employment. If all wages rose equally with the same impact on prices, except for a questionable short-run loss of employment the magnitude of which would depend upon the ease with which capital can be substituted for labor in production, the effect on employment should be neutral, i.e., total employment would be unchanged. Inflation would result were there no change in income distribution toward labor, and aggregate demand would remain unaltered.

But in reality, all wages do not move in unison. With different degrees of union pressure, and a large unorganized sector of labor, wage push is applied unevenly throughout the economy. Therefore, with variable price changes, although total demand might remain unchanged, demand would tend to shift toward those goods whose prices rose relatively the least.

Cost Push and Sectoral Shifts in Demand

According to one variant of the cost-push theory, sectoral shifts in demand are prime movers in the inflation process. With total demand remaining unchanged, the prices of certain goods tend to rise as demand for them increases. Meanwhile, in those sectors which suffer a decline in demand, prices fail to fall, either because the prices of these goods are administered in monopolistic markets and do not respond automatically in accordance with the textbook efficiency of freely operating markets, or because they are forced upward by rising wages. This wage push results from the efforts of other workers to match the wage gains secured by the workers in the sector enjoying the increase in demand.

This inflation theory might be considered an offshoot of the demand-pull school in that the inflation begins with a shift in demand. A change in the composition of total demand, however, might have resulted from differential wage pushes without changes in demand schedules. A change in the internal pattern of total demand could follow the pattern of differential wage and price changes in different sectors. Starting with an autonomous shift in demand, a rise in wages and prices could result in one sector, and this rise could elicit further shifts of demand.

Under the first variant, wages and prices would be higher in the sector which instituted the wage push; in the other case wages and prices would be higher in the sector experiencing the autonomous increase in demand. In either case, the inflation results because of the downward inflexibility in prices in the sector losing demand, whether because of a self-imposed rise in wages and prices or because of an autonomous shift in demand to another sector. In both instances, unemployment tends to appear in the sector of declining demand.

This theory explains how unemployment can arise from a sectoral shift in demand without a preceding decline in aggregate demand. Of course, the severity and duration of unemployment depends on the ability of the displaced workers in the sector of declining demand to find employment in the expanding sector. By the middle of 1958 unemployment had increased to 5.4 million, the highest level since before World War II. Whether this unemployment resulted from sectoral shifts or from a general decline in aggregate demand is debatable. If the latter were the true cause, the accompanying inflation might be explained on the following grounds.

During the months of rising unemployment of 1957–1958, the

full-employment policy of the government must be considered to have been unsuccessful. Nevertheless, the level of personal income was maintained and even increased during the period, partly because of increases in government transfer payments. Thus, while the unemployed were no longer producing goods and services, the total amount of income available for buying consumer items had increased. In effect, government policy of maintaining purchasing power under conditions of declining supply resulting from the downturn in production might have been responsible for a short-term demand-pull inflation during the brief recession.

Cost Push and Markup Pricing

Most inflation theories are concerned with the initial phase of the inflation process. Whether demand-pull or cost-push, these theories offer detailed explanation of the operation of inflationary forces but usually assume that the spiral of costs chasing prices, or vice versa, continues in some indefinite way through the operation of the market system. One theory holds that, regardless of the nature of the initial pull or push, the process continues not through the operation of competitive markets but through adjustments in the monopolistic pricing of final goods and productive services. Under such pricing, both management and labor use the markup technique. If demand pull raises prices, then labor will mark up its wages to protect its share of total product. On the other hand, if wages rise, management will raise prices to adjust its markup to previous levels. Thus, in a staggered series of rising wages and prices, set administratively rather than through the functioning of current market supply and demand forces, inflation continues in an endless process until outside forces check the upward movement.

Cost Push and Productivity

In the absence of any improvement in productive efficiency, under cost-push conditions profits can rise without leading to inflation only if returns to other factors of production are reduced. Similarly, if wages rise, prices must also rise unless there is a reduction in profits and a redistribution of income toward labor. If, however, an improvement in productive efficiency takes place, then both profits and wages can rise without a resulting price increase. Presumably, if productivity, measured by output per man-hour, rises by 3 per cent, then wage rates may rise by 3 per cent, the returns to other factors also increase by 3 per cent, and the level of prices remains constant. The gain in productivity would thereby be shared as an equivalent gain in real and money income for all factors, given a constant level of total demand. Alternatively, the gain in real income could take the form of price reductions provided factor costs did not rise.

Thus, "responsible" wage policy, according to cost-push theorists, can be defined as one in which wage demands do not exceed the improvement in productivity, since such a policy would not create upward pressure on prices. On the other hand, "irresponsible" wage policy would be one in which wage demands, measured as a percentage increase over current levels, exceeded the percentage improvement in productivity. A refined cost-push theory states that a wage-push inflation results from wage increases that exceed the permissible level consistent with stable prices, that is, exceed the productivity improvement.

Attempts to measure whether wage policy has been responsible or not usually involve the comparative study of wage and productivity movements. The table on page xvi presents the changes in money wages, real wages, and productivity in manufacturing since the end of World War II.

Examination of the table below reveals a tendency for money wages to rise faster than productivity gains. From 1947 to 1958 money wages increased relatively more than productivity for each year except 1950 and 1955. Money wages advanced by 73.7 per cent from 1947 to 1958 while productivity increased only 32.2 per cent over the period. The gap narrowed only slightly between 1958 and 1961. Insofar as money wages rose autonomously, then the data offer support to the cost-push thesis; wages outpaced the non-inflationary gains permitted by productivity improvement. The data do not reveal, however, that the wage increases were autonomous. Perhaps the movement was from price increases to wage increases.

By comparing real wage changes with productivity movements it is possible to learn whether labor's share increased during the period. This comparison reveals a close parallel in movement of the two variables. From 1947 through 1958 real wages increased 34.2 per cent, compared with the 32.2 per cent total gain in productivity. Real wages increased relatively more than productivity in five of the eleven years and relatively less in six. Only during the last three years studied, 1958–1961, when the wide productivity gains were not matched by equivalent increases in real wages, did the overall figures yield a lag in real wages.

Comparisons between money wages and productivity or between real wages and productivity can lead to false conclusions about the

WAGES AND PRODUCTIVITY IN MANUFACTURING, 1947–1961

Year	Average Hourly Earnings (Straight Time)	Consumer Price Index (1957–59 = 100)	Average Real Wages[1]	Output per Man-Hour[2] (1957–59 = 100)	Annual % Change (× 100)		
					Average Hourly Earnings	Average Real Wages	Output per Man-Hour
1947	$1.18	77.8	$1.52	74.8	....	....	....
1948	1.29	83.8	1.54	76.8	109.3	101.3	102.7
1949	1.34	83.0	1.61	78.5	103.9	104.5	102.2
1950	1.39	83.8	1.66	83.7	103.7	103.1	106.6
1951	1.51	90.5	1.67	85.2	108.6	100.6	101.8
1952	1.59	92.5	1.72	86.4	105.3	103.0	101.4
1953	1.68	93.2	1.80	90.6	105.7	104.7	104.9
1954	1.73	93.6	1.85	89.8	103.0	102.8	99.1
1955	1.79	93.3	1.92	96.0	103.5	103.8	106.9
1956	1.89	94.7	2.00	97.1	105.6	104.2	101.1
1957	1.99	98.0	2.03	97.2	105.3	101.5	100.1
1958	2.05	100.7	2.04	98.9	103.0	100.5	101.7
1959	2.12	101.5	2.09	103.7	103.4	102.5	104.9
1960	2.20	103.1	2.13	106.1	103.8	101.9	102.3
1961	2.25	104.2	2.16	110.7	102.3	101.4	104.3
Ratio 1958/1947 (× 100)	173.7		134.2	132.2			
Ratio 1961/1947 (× 100)	190.7		142.1	148.0			

Source: Bureau of Labor Statistics. Although manufacturing represents only a part of the total economy, it is usually this sector to which cost-push inflation is attributed.

[1] Money wages deflated by the Consumer Price Index (Col. 2 ÷ Col. 3)

[2] Output per man-hour of production workers does not measure the contribution of labor alone, but represents the improvement in productive efficiency that can be attributed to more and better capital equipment, and new productive techniques, as well as improvements in labor efficiency itself. As such, it is only a crude measurement of the gain in labor efficiency in isolation. Its accuracy depends on the closeness of the gain in labor efficiency to all other improvements.

causes of the inflation. The data can only show that labor does or does not improve its relative position, measured by its share of total product. They do not indicate whether or not the inflationary process is initiated by labor's attempts to improve its position through wage increases. The inflationary process might begin with a wage push which is met by a rise in prices just sufficient to restore the balance between wages and returns to other factors.

Wage-productivity data cannot, therefore, reveal the prime cause of inflation, whether demand pull or wage push, or even profit push in cases where a price increase prior to a wage rise does not result from an increase in the level of aggregate demand. While it is a valid contention that a wage increase in excess of a productivity improvement will create inflationary pressure, historical data in isolation cannot show whether this excess was the cause or result of an accompanying price rise. To ask labor to confine its wage increases to productivity gains in a period of rising prices is to ask it to suffer a decline in real wages and its relative share of national income in the interest of stemming an inflation begun by other forces.

Inflation Remedies

Suggestions for controlling or preventing inflation are related to the nature of the inflation. When demand pull is considered the cause, the program for effective control is quite simple. If the monetary and fiscal authorities impose anti-inflationary measures of credit limitation, interest rate increases, and higher taxes, the excess demand that created and prolonged the inflation will be eliminated.

The simplicity of demand-pull remedies arises from the impersonal nature of the causal factor. Market forces induce the inflation and it is only necessary to divert or reduce these forces to remove the pressure. On the other hand, cost-push inflation does not arise from the involved workings of the market mechanism. It stems from the arbitrary desire of business leaders, in the case of profit push, or of labor leaders, in the case of wage push, to increase their share of the total income by means of raising the price of their products and services. It is obviously unrealistic to suggest that a vague plea for restraint in profit or wage demands would be effective as a means of eliminating cost-push inflationary pressure. However, a formula for limiting profit and wage demands, especially the latter, to gains in productivity has had wide acceptance as a noninflationary policy. In 1962 the Council of Economic Advisors suggested as a Wage Guidepost for limiting inflation that the rate of wage increases equal the rate of productivity growth. The formula relates to wage policy under conditions of stable prices, thus making it clear that any wage increases beyond the productivity gain would be an obvious example of a wage-push labor practice.

The Council did not advise that wages match productivity growth industry by industry. Such a formula would distort wage structure since workers, perhaps within the same skill classification, would receive substantially different wages depending on the productivity experiences of their particular industries. Instead, the Council suggested that all wage adjustments be tied to the national average productivity increase.

Following this Guidepost would lead to a national average increase in wages equal to the average productivity gain. For those industries having a greater productivity increase than the national level, unit labor costs would fall and the Guidepost would call for price declines. For the industries in which productivity rose less than the national average, prices would have to rise in response to increased unit labor costs. An important criticism of the Guidepost is that it recommends transferring the disequilibrium in the labor market, which would have occurred had wage changes been related to productivity movements industry by industry, to the product market by allowing differential price adjustments to stabilize the general price level. The economy is in a state of continual change, if not overall at least among sectors. If an industry has improved its productivity position while suffering a downturn in demand, then any wage increase might lead to unemployment. On the other hand, another industry experiencing an increase in demand might not clear the market for its goods if, in accordance with the Guidepost, its price fell because of a better-than-average gain in productivity; demand would soon exceed supply. Pricing under the Guidepost would not be determined by market forces, but by compliance with a formula that assumed rigid market conditions. Although theoretically the level of aggregate demand would remain unchanged, the presence of excess demand in some areas and excess supply in others would only aggravate the disequilibrium already evident in our current economy.

Further argument against the Guidepost may be found in the condition of unchanging income distribution which strict compliance entails. The share of wages and profits would remain unchanged, and although historically there has been constancy in labor's share of total income, it is doubtful whether labor leaders would want to be tied to a policy that guaranteed a continued constant share. Moreover, by treating all labor equally, the Guidepost would perpetuate the present wage structure. Variable movements in wage differentials are a part of our wage history, and again it is doubtful that a national policy which froze occupational, skill, and regional differentials at their present relationships would find much popular support within labor itself.

The Impact of Inflation

Economists are not in agreement on whether the overall effects of inflation are harmful or beneficial to a country. Distributional shifts in income depend on the relationship of money income increases to the price rise. Of course, those with fixed or relatively stable incomes suffer a real income loss during inflation, while those whose incomes rise faster than prices gain in real income. Similarly, debtors who pay off money contracts made when prices were low have the advantage over creditors who receive repayment in money of low purchasing power.

There is theoretical argument about the relative changes in real income of capital and labor during an inflation. The Keynesian theory of economic expansion rests partly on the assumption that prices will outrun money wages as aggregate demand increases. Workers, deluded by a "money illusion," permit this reduction in real wages, which in turn facilitates the increase in production. According to this theory, in the short run real wages must fall when capital remains fixed and labor costs rise as output increases. If real wages did not fall, producers would have no incentive to increase production, and the tendency toward a higher level of economic activity would be thwarted in its beginning.

This theory rests on the assumption that capital is the bottleneck in attempts to increase output. For the United States, except for the immediate post-World War II period when real wages in fact did fall as prices and production rose, this assumption is unrealistic. Labor and capital are in joint productive demand, and the reemployment of idle plant and equipment as well as idle men during business expansions makes the presence of bottlenecks, whether of capital or labor, questionable. Statistical studies of the comparative movement of prices and money wages have proved inconclusive. Some studies of the recovery years of the 1930's showed that although money wages rose along with output and employment, real wages fell as prices rose faster than wages. Other studies showed a rise in real wages. In any case, these studies of recovery from a low level of economic activity are not applicable to situations of economic growth from a position of nearly full employment.

The nature of bottlenecks in advanced economies is uncertain, but for many developing countries it is more certain that capital shortages are the bottlenecks to economic growth. With surplus agricultural population and a general scarcity of capital equipment, many economists in these countries consider that the success of economic progress, at least in the private sector, depends on a rising rate of capital return and a decline in real wages. A school of opinion on inflation called "structuralism" has appeared among central planners of Latin American countries. Structuralists believe that inflation is a natural consequence of the development process stemming from structural bottlenecks, perhaps in the import sector of the balance of payments, perhaps in the supply of materials and capital currently available for growth. The outcome of inflation, structuralists maintain, is a rise in the real rate of profit and a decline in the real wage rate, which strengthens activity in the sphere of private investment. Further stimulus to private investment comes from the rise in the real rate of profit compared to the real rate of interest, which tends to fall insofar as relatively fixed interest charges face rising prices. Structuralists believe that efforts to stabilize the price level only check these expansionary forces acting on investment and thus retard economic development.

Opposed to the structuralists are the "monetarists" who believe that price stabilization will create a climate favorable to development. They point to the critical balance of payments problem that would result from following structuralist policy and note the recent political discontent and upheaval in countries where uncontrolled inflation disrupted economic life. Monetarists believe in rigid monetary controls, if necessary, to prevent the inflation which development tends to create.

In general there are political overtones to the structuralist and monetarist views. Adherents to structuralism take what some consider a leftist or an ultranationalistic view of economic development. Structuralists look for development to come about entirely from the resources of the country itself, without regard to the reduction in import capacity or discouragement of foreign investment that results from inflation. Monetarists, on the other hand, while admitting the need for internal effort in the development process, are concerned not only with the continued political stability of the country, but also with maintaining a favorable climate for foreign investment and tourism and with strengthening import capacity.

The literature of inflation contains countless books and articles of varying professional degree, from emotional diatribes against organized labor or big business to refined theoretical models of the inflation process. The writings selected for this book have been chosen on the basis of their reputations as leading expositions of the important theories and points of view described above.

Morton's "Trade Unionism, Full Employment and Inflation" is one of the best known postwar presentations of the demand-pull thesis. After the lifting of price controls and well before the creeping inflation, the demand-pull position was substantiated by economic experience. Morton's main contribution was his stress on the importance of government action during the postwar inflation, whether through its passive monetary policy or its support of full employment as a national goal.

The next two selections, excerpts from Schultze's paper before the Joint Economic Committee, "Recent Inflation in the United States," and Ackley's paper before the same committee, "A Third Approach to the Analysis and Control of Inflation," offer specialized variants of the cost-push position. Schultze is the chief exponent of the sectoral shift approach to the inflationary process, while Ackley originated the markup pricing thesis of the continuation of inflationary forces. As was noted earlier, both theses contain demand-pull elements, but only to the extent of the initial cause of inflation. Both depend on a form of cost push for the inflation to continue. In Schultze's opinion, the failure of wages and prices to fall in the sector of declining demand actually leads to the rise in the overall price level. Ackley holds that the continual upward movement of administered prices and wages propels prices upward once inflation has begun, whatever its cause.

The Wage Guidepost has been criticized for its built-in rigidity and for its difficulty of application. In addition, Machlup in his "Another View of Cost-Push and Demand-Pull Inflation," presents the argument that any policy which ties wage increases to productivity gains is inherently inflationary. While Machlup confines his study to the policy of granting productivity gains to the factors employed in the industries in which the gains occur, his analysis also applies to a policy of granting identical wage increases in all industries based on the average national growth in productivity — the policy of the Guidepost.

Economic theories are generally born of economic experience. Therefore, since almost all previous inflations had been obviously associated with demand-pull conditions, such as wars and political upheavals, cost-push theories did not become prevalent until the creeping inflation of the late 1950's, when demand-pull elements were less evident. Thus, Thorp and Quandt called their book *The New Inflation* to encompass all theories that post-date the approach to the causes of inflation based on the quantity theory of money. The chapter selected deals with the relationship of inflation to economic growth. In it the authors note some of the stimulating features of inflation on growth — those which mainly affect incentives to invest. While their frame of reference is the American economy, lagging wage increases relative to the rise in profit rates, and the increase in the profit rate relative to the rate of interest probably have more applicability to economic development in backward economies than to growth in advanced ones.

Continuing the theme of the effects of inflation on development, De Oliveira Campos' paper, "Two Views on Inflation in Latin America," reviews the structuralist and monetarist positions. While he takes no side in the debate, he does raise the point that, even granting the structuralist conclusion that monetary stabilization retards investment, long-term growth might not be thereby retarded. The improved composition of investment resulting from price stability would aid growth more than inflation-induced speculative investments.

[In the following selections many footnotes, mainly bibliographical, have been omitted. Tables and graphs have been renumbered for consistency in presentation.]

INFLATION
Demand-Pull or Cost-Push?

PART ONE

THE CASE FOR DEMAND PULL

WALTER A. MORTON

Trade Unionism,
Full Employment and Inflation*

Like most pioneering efforts, Morton's theories now appear obvious. However, it is the mark of the influence of significant contributions that they are studied and reviewed to such an extent that the novelty of the original presentation is forgotten. Certainly the concept of demand-pull inflation and the implied influence of money supply on the price level antedates Morton's paper. In fact, it has its origins in the quantity theory of money. Morton's originality was in the role he gave to monetary and fiscal policy in the inflationary process.

While demand pull might have been the source of the underlying inflationary pressure of the period following World War II, Morton emphasized that it was the monetary and fiscal authorities who made that potential power effective in raising prices. The monetary authorities, in passively permitting increases in the money supply or in failing to restrict credit or to impose upward pressure on interest rates, permitted a situation of excess demand and excess money seeking a

* Reprinted by permission of the American Economic Association: Walter A. Morton, "Trade Unionism, Full Employment and Inflation," *American Economic Review*, XL (March 1950), pp. 13–39.

limited supply of goods. The fiscal authorities, by their comparatively neutral tax policy, failed to stem the outflow of demand released after four years of wartime restraint.

Further, the support, albeit indefinite, of a full-employment policy which came from the Employment Act of 1946 indicated to labor and management that, regardless of the recklessness of their wage and price policies, the government would shield them from the danger of unemployment and the threat of reduced sales. While Morton did not oppose government action in cases of general unemployment and business depression, he labeled inflationary a policy which readjusted the employment and output balance in sectors where autonomous wage and price policies, based on the knowledge of the government's balancing role, were causing disequilibrium in a downward direction.

Morton's recommendations for preventing inflation place a heavy responsibility on the monetary and fiscal authorities. Monetary controls have powerful influences on the economy. While trying to prevent inflation by restricting credit and putting upward pressure on interest rates—the means of limiting money supply—monetary authorities run the risk of overcompensating for the inflation and setting depressionary forces in motion. Large-scale changes in interest rates and credit, required to weaken a strong inflation, are bound to damage the economic position of certain firms and industries by reducing their borrowing capacity.

Furthermore, in these days of increasing use of internal funds and new bond or stock issues, it is doubtful whether controls operating mainly through the banking system would have the desired effect of significantly reducing inflationary pressure. The strength of the restrictions would have to be greater than in past periods of more general reliance on bank borrowing. Since large firms are turning away from the use of bank funds, any negative effects on the economy resulting from a restrictive monetary policy would tend to fall on small businesses which still rely heavily on bank borrowing for funds and which can least afford a weakening in their borrowing capacity. Finally, even if the money supply were reduced by monetary policy, there would be no guarantee that inflationary pressure would be equivalently diminished. Past inflations show that increased velocity of money can compensate for sluggish increases in total money supply.

The depressionary effects of restrictive fiscal moves to stem inflation are obvious. Tax increases act directly to reduce purchasing power and indirectly to retard investment.

While a policy of strict monetary controls and higher taxes may lead to results that harm the economy more than inflation, this cannot reflect on the validity of Morton's position. He was mainly interested in the causes of inflation and not in the issue of the overall results of measures preventing or eliminating it. In defense of his presentation it might be argued that his almost total denial of the importance of cost-push factors can be excused since he was describing the historical events of the post World War II inflation, a period in which even the most rigid cost-push adherents would admit the presence of excess demand.

In fairness to his critics, however, it must be acknowledged that Morton does at times extrapolate his description of the post-war inflation into a general statement of inflation theory. To accept his statement that

Business inflations, moreover, instead of being inaugurated by wage demands, come from optimistic expectations and bank borrowings which raise prices ahead of wages. The need for additional credits to pay higher wages has not, and is not likely to become the initiating force in credit expansion because no individual producer can act on the assumption that his own market will be expanded by an increase in his own payrolls. It seems unlikely, therefore, that labor can alter the traditional wage lag into a wage lead.

is to deny the existence of wage-push inflation, or to relegate to irrelevancy half the literature on inflation.

As a result of the postwar experience the belief has grown that one of the strongest impediments to the use of monetary and fiscal powers for the maintenance of a high national income is the increased strength of trade unions and their influence over the wage level. It is feared that trade union policy will compel a continued annual increase in wage rates exceeding the rise in physical productivity, thus making price inflation a necessary concomitant of full employment and forcing the unpalatable alternative of underemployment or inflation. We shall, therefore, inquire into the influence of unionism in the past and what it is likely to be in the future.

I

Although not always clearly formulated, the alleged inflationary influence of unionism can be reduced to three propositions.

(1) That trade unions in the postwar period have pursued policies that made the rise in prices much greater than it would have been with individual bargaining and competition in the labor market, and that this policy was made possible by the fact that unionism is a form of monopoly power which is inherently inflationary. This view implicitly assumes that except for unionism, prices would have risen much less and that the wage-price spiral would not have existed under the assumed conditions of perfect competition in the labor market. Wage policies are looked upon as the instigator and principal cause rather than the instrument of the wage-price spiral.

(2) That if unions had pursued a policy of money wage stabilization instead of trying to keep wages abreast of prices, the degree of inflation would have been less. This view does not contrast actual policies with the assumed results of perfect competition but rather with a sacrificial wage policy in which the leadership deliberately sacrificed possible wage gains in order to keep prices down. It assumes such policies were possible for the leadership and would have been more beneficial to the community.

(3) That the wage-price spiral could have been prevented if unions had exerted their political influence to retain wage and price control in 1946 instead of asking for the discard of the Little Steel Formula and the determination of wages by voluntary collective action. This is a criticism of labor politics and beyond our purview here where we are dealing with labor policy in a free market.

Those who believe that unionism is inherently inflationary propose that we prepare to suffer its consequences or destroy the unions. Some suggest a drastic change in the allocation of economic power by restoration of atomistic competition and liberalism of the purported nineteenth-century type which they fancy will make our system function more effectively. They would apply the traditional American anti-monopoly philosophy to trade unions which have heretofore been exempt from it. A second group assumes that no substantial change will occur in our institutions, but they believe that unions might pursue better policies, putting their faith in reason, exhortation, intimidation and economic coercion mixed in uncertain proportions. A third group believing that unionism is here to stay but that the self-interest of unions is and will remain incompatible with stability of prices and full employment, advocate direct governmental control over the general level of wages through national wage policy enforced by law or custom as a substitute for the determination of wage levels by voluntary collective bargaining. We shall examine these proposals after we have considered the causes of the recent price spiral and the part played therein by organized labor.

II

The recent inflation is unique because it has resulted predominantly from an increase in the velocity of money whereas in previous inflations prices, wages, and the quantity of money moved upward together. We might also characterize it as a delayed effect of the wartime increase in the money supply which had been temporarily dammed up by price control. The process of inflation was the wage-price, expenditure-income spiral. The basic causes were the quantity of money and a persistent demand for goods. In this view the spiral is not an independent, alternative explanation of price changes which can be substituted for the monetary theory; it is merely a description of inflationary processes which fits into the framework of traditional theory. By so treating it we can integrate the mechanism of inflation with the quantity theory of money by means of income-expenditure analysis. The recent treatment of the spiral as an independent causal explanation is, moreover, misleading for policy purposes because it mistakes the instrumentality by which inflation occurs for its causes and puts emphasis upon direct legal regulation of wages and prices rather than on monetary and fiscal control of the quantity and velocity of money. There is, however, a simple explanation for this elevation of a process into a first principle. Because we had given up hope of controlling the dammed up inflation after the war by reducing the quantity of money or lowering its velocity by drastic taxation, we tried to stop the spiral by exhorting and threatening labor and business. As a consequence, the erroneous belief grew that the level of prices is determined by the spiral, and primary attention was directed to the wage bargain and to profits rather than to the quantity of money.[1]

[1] This emphasis upon the process of inflation to the neglect of its basic cause in an excessive money supply appears to be a direct consequent of recent preoccupation with the income-expenditure theory of output and prices. The simple quantity theorists tended to attribute price fluctuations to the monetary

At the close of the war the supply of money was ample to sustain a rise in prices and its velocity was low by all past standards.[2]

factor without examining the underlying economic and psychological conditions responsible for changes in quantity and velocity. The simple income theorists, on the other hand, attribute price fluctuations to changes in income without examining the influence of the quantity of money. Is such exclusiveness really necessary? The depression years showed the possibility of fluctuations in expenditure without alterations in the amount of money, but it is sheer myopia not to see that since 1940 the greatly enlarged money supply throughout the world is the primary reason for larger incomes and higher prices. The error of the traditional quantity theory persisting through Irving Fisher was threefold: (1) It did not explain the underlying economic facts and expectations responsible for expansion and contraction in the volume of circulating media and its velocity. (2) It assumed velocity to be constant. (3) It did not explicitly show the process by which money affected prices through its effect on income. Recent income-expenditure analysis attempts to remedy the first two deficiencies by analyzing the causes of business fluctuations and it supplies the third need with the Keynesian formula $Y = C + I$. Substitute MV (income velocity) for Y, and PT for $C + I$, and the relationships are apparent. In utilizing the income theory, we need not therefore minimize the great contribution of the quantity theory and the light which it has thrown on general price changes throughout history, nor should we discard the experience of centuries that changes in the quantity of money have been the most important single cause of depreciation in its value.

Professor Alvin Hansen, however, in presenting the income theory sets up an opposition between it and the quantity theory saying: "It is the volume of expenditures, not the quantity of money, to which primary attention must be given," Monetary Theory and Fiscal Policy, Alvin H. Hansen (New York, 1949), p. 83. We must agree that the total of MV is more significant than M alone or V alone but it does not seem possible either a priori or from experience to say whether it is M or V that is always more important. Here we need recourse to the concepts of limiting and strategic factors (Institutional Economics, John R. Commons, [New York, 1933], p. 89). In depression V seems to be the strategic factor; to prevent a boom M must be controlled by the monetary authority. Hansen shows the inclination to minimize the importance of the quantity of money in quoting Keynes: "According to the quantity theory, if you first 'let out your belt' you will in consequence of this action necessarily grow fat!" (p. 85). This is a good criticism of the unfounded belief of Warren in 1933 that increasing the number of gold dollars would automatically raise prices, or for that matter, of any belief that money acts upon prices directly regardless of the willingness to spend, or without affecting incomes through consumption and investment, but it is of limited value to explain inflation. Looking back at the trend of prices since 1914, in the United States and Western Europe, I wonder how many would deny that the quantity of money was primary in monetary depreciation; or that it has been so since the last war in much of the world. We let out our monetary belt and prices rose! And if we had not let it out prices and incomes would not have risen anywhere near as much.

[2] For a summary statement on supply of money and liquid assets see Statement of Marriner S. Eccles, Chairman, Board of Governors, Federal Reserve System, Hearing before the Joint Committee on the Economic Report, Nov. 25, 1947

This inflationary monetary potential was able to support the 50 per cent rise in wholesale prices which took place from the end of price control in the spring of 1946 to the summer of 1948 and is still capable of supporting a further inflation. During this period the Treasury paid off bank debts of approximately 9 billion dollars but this was offset by an approximately equal expansion of member bank loans which the Federal Reserve System could not prevent because of its policy of supporting the government bond market. Interpreting the effect of this increase in the money supply according to the strict quantity theory, it could be held responsible for about 10 per cent of the price rise. But the actual effect was most likely greater than 10 per cent, because these funds were placed in strategic hands and probably had a greater velocity than the rest of demand deposits. Bankers, however, contend that these loans were not inflationary because they were used to overcome bottlenecks, to supply deficiencies, and otherwise to augment the supply of goods which, they contend, with considerable merit, was ultimately deflationary. On the whole, however, there is little doubt that the predominant cause of inflation was not treasury policy or bank policy but the release of idle balances to satisfy a pent-up demand for goods, raising prices, creating full employment, and with it an increased demand for labor which enabled workers to win wage increases.

Because of the lag of wages behind the cost of living, labor leaders contend that higher wages did not cause higher prices but were caused by them. This argument is only half correct. The wage effect was twofold: the pushing or cost effect, and the pulling or demand effect. Increased wages raise marginal costs and hence the price at which output can be supplied. The labor leaders are correct in so far as wage increases as costs did not push up prices; prices were pulled up by a market demand great enough to absorb the entire output at prices yielding substantial profits. In industries operating under competition, wage increases were mainly excuses for price increases, not their cause. In these industries, of which agriculture, cotton textiles, and meat packing are striking examples, prices would have been the same even under the supposititious case that wages were paid by the government and wage costs to the manufacturer had been zero; or to state it less strikingly but more realistically, even if wage costs to the

(Washington, 1948), and Senate Report No. 1565, *High Prices of Consumer Goods* (Washington, 1948), p. 29. The velocity of deposits between 1921 and 1929 in one hundred leading cities ranged between 21 and 23. It fell to lower levels in the 1930's ranging between 13 and 19. In 1945 it was only 9.7; in 1946, 10.0; in 1947, 12.0; and in 1948, 12.9.

icer had been much less than they actually were. Changes in
ge costs cannot therefore account for changes in the prices of
competitive goods sold at equilibrium prices during the inflationary
period.

They were, however, an important factor in regulated industry
such as railroads and electric utilities where increased costs had to be
compensated by higher rates; and in industries pursuing "price policies" based on costs which induced them to "underprice" their output. Steel is a notable example of the latter. Subject to these modifi-
cations, labor's contention that the "cost effect" did not raise prices is
largely correct. Not so, however, the demand effect.

Higher payrolls raised prices because they increased the total
demand for goods. Payrolls rose because of both greater employment
and higher wages. Professor Sumner H. Slichter shows that between
1945 and 1947 increased demand due to higher wages accounts for
only about one-half of the increase in prices, the other half being
attributable to greater employment, and the expenditures of other
groups.[3] Higher payrolls raised the price of farm products and helped
sustain the higher price level at which manufactured goods had to
be sold. As these prices rose, labor again asked for a second and then
a third round which continued to have the same results. The excessive cash holdings were thus translated first into consumer demand,
then into higher prices, then into higher wages and incomes, and
again into demand, prices, incomes, expenditures and so on in the
manner described. Forces other than labor also contributing to the
inflation were the higher incomes and expenditures of farmers, pro-
prietors and other high-income groups, the eagerness to procure goods,
dishoarding, reduction in the proportion of savings, the growth of
consumer credit, expenditures for new plant and equipment, the
growth in mortgage debt on urban real estate, and large federal and
local expenditures for domestic and international purposes.

The wage-price spiral was, therefore, a cause of inflation but not
the sole cause nor even a sufficient cause to bring about the degree
of price change that has taken place. More properly the spiral might
be designated as an income-expenditure spiral. And finally, as will
be shown, the wage-price spiral is not an exclusive product of unionism but has existed in every inflation regardless of the organization
of the labor market and would have existed in the contemporary
scene even had there been a competitive labor market.

[3] *Higher Payrolls Raised the Price of Farm Wages and Prices,* An address
before the Academy of Political Science, Columbia University, Vol. XXIII,
No. 1 (May 1948), pp. 50–51.

There is no reason to believe that prices would have risen less even if labor unions had been weak or nonexistent. Labor unions were a negligible factor in our previous great inflations — that of the American Revolutionary War, the War of 1812, the Civil War, and World War I. Nor have they been a predominant factor in the European inflations following the first world war or those in Hungary, Austria, Germany, Italy, France, China or Japan after the last war. Past experience shows that even in a competitive labor market wages rise along with prices, subject to lag, in any price spiral.

It might even be contended with considerable justification that the existence of organized labor has been an anti-inflationary force in so far as it created a fear of future wage rigidity and thus caused employers to resist the upward movement in wages and prices. Many administered prices were deliberately kept down below equilibrium market prices. Manufacturers seemed to have been motivated in this by the desire to maintain business stability, to retain consumer good will, to prevent public intervention, and to keep their wage costs and prices at a long-run equilibrium level. The expected rigidity of wage rates in face of a future fall in demand, along with these other factors, operated to keep prices and wages lower than they might have been under competition. In a completely competitive economy with producers and workers both seeking to maximize immediate money gain, the upward spiral would probably have been faster and prices higher than in the present regimen of a mixture of monopoly and competition.

Accordingly, it seems reasonable to offer the following conclusions regarding the effect of unionism on prices. (1) The wage-price spiral has always existed, with or without unionism. (2) Wages as a cost did not markedly influence market prices of goods sold under competition. (3) In so far as the selling prices of many important manufactures were less than equilibrium prices and producers were governed by the notion of a "reasonable" profit, wage costs had some influence on administered prices of "monopolists." (4) Wage costs also affected governmentally regulated prices. (5) Under conditions of "perfect competition" throughout the economy, prices would probably have risen faster but wages would have lagged. (6) Assuming monopolistic competition among producers but perfect competition among workers (the position of the anti-unionists), prices would have risen but wages would have lagged even more. (7) Fear of wage rigidity in the slump was one of the reasons that "monopolistic" producers kept prices and wages lower than they might have been in a competitive labor market. (8) The net influence of trade unionism has been to reduce the wage lag somewhat, but its effect on competitive prices has been negligible and its effect on administered prices, though obscure, appears to have been two-fold, to raise these prices as wages rose but to keep them from rising as high as they might have done had producers not feared future effects of wage rigidity.

III

Let us now consider the effect of a changed distribution of income, whether brought about by trade unionism or any other cause, upon the level of prices by operation on the demand side of the equation. The price-output effect will depend in the first instance upon the way in which such a change affects the composition of and the total expenditure. Labor leaders contended in 1947 that the wage lag at that time would bring about underconsumption, failure of demand, lower investment, lower prices and depression. They were supported in this Hobsonian or maldistributionist theory by the Americans for Democratic Action.[4] The argument that higher wages increase total demand was, however, Janus faced, and was accepted also by those who blamed labor for the inflation and opposed further wage increases. Both of these views were erroneous at the time they were presented, for aggregate demand was already excessive at the existing price level, and prices were bound to rise whether in response to the demands of workers or of other segments of the population. The diversion of income away from labor would have altered the composition but not the total amount of expenditure: it might have created a smaller rise in the prices of foods and clothing, but probably would have increased corporate outlay for plant and equipment and would not have lessened the demand for machinery, steel, automobiles, refrigerators and other goods in demand by all groups of the population, and being bought not only out of income but out of savings and by the creation of new debt. Lower wages or a wage lag would simply have given a larger share of total output to others.

The theory of income maldistribution was nevertheless used by labor to attack high corporate profits, cited as a cause of impending depression and as a reason for wage increases, abolition of excise taxes and reduction in income taxes on the lower brackets. Opponents to this program, on the other hand, held that greater profits were

4 See Testimony of Leon Henderson, *Current Price Developments and the Problem of Economic Stabilization, Hearings before the Joint Committee on the Economic Report, Eightieth Congress, July 16, 1947,* p. 477 and ff.

necessary to stimulate further capital investment and thus to maintain employment. Both groups argued for more stimulation of monetary demand, when less was needed. Under the circumstances, it was the classical theory that was more appropriate; real capital investment could only be promoted by diverting resources from consumption goods to capital goods, and a real increase in consumption could be obtained only by decreasing investment. The attempt to increase one without the sacrifice of the other resulted in further monetary inflation. Whatever may be the truth of the underconsumptionist doctrine for some periods of the cycle or of the secular trend, it was obviously irrelevant during the years 1946 to 1948. Likewise, the doctrine that more monetary investment was desirable was also inadequate and misleading unless it was coupled with the proviso that it should be attained through decreased consumption. This raises the general issue whether the distribution of income has any effect at all, at any time, on the general level of prices.

During the 1930's it was widely accepted that a shift of income from the rich to the poor was favorable to employment because it resulted in increased consumption, decreased saving, and increased investment opportunities. More recently it has been said, on the contrary, that such a redistribution can have little effect on consumption because the marginal propensity to consume is about the same at all income levels.[5] Hence a change of income from an upper bracket to a lower bracket brought about by taxation or by wage increases has practically no effect on consumption and saving and hence none on total expenditure.[6] Whether this is true cannot be settled except

[5] Harold Lubell, "Effects of Income Redistribution on Consumer Expenditures," *Am. Econ. Rev.*, Vol. XXXVII, No. 1 (March 1947), p. 157, and Correction, *Am. Econ. Rev.*, Vol. XXXVII, No. 5 (December 1947), p. 930; also J. M. Clark, *ibid.*, p. 931.

[6] This proposition refers only to individual incomes, not to shifts in income from individuals to corporations. A cut in taxes on low incomes compensated by increased corporate taxes would be a form of income-redistribution which would increase consumption since the marginal propensity of individuals to consume is higher than that of corporations, which is zero. So, also, a wage increase at the expense of corporate profits. This is true because only a part of corporate profits is redistributed to stockholders and made available for consumption; the balance remains as surplus and is either invested in plant or kept as a liquid asset. Whatever, therefore, may be true of the consumption effect of interpersonal income redistribution is probably not true of redistribution between persons and corporations so long as corporate dividends remain only a fraction (at present about a half) of profits. When they reach parity, then the rôle of the corporate entity may be neglected for this problem.

Both Lubell and Clark (citation note 5) also neglect the differential rates of

by further data and analysis, but we may postulate it and explore its implications.

It follows from its postulate that the theory that higher wages are stimulating to consumption is invalid, that such a shift does not affect total consumption but merely causes a change in its composition; instead of necessities bought by the lower-income groups, luxuries are bought by the higher-income groups. Consequently, whatever justification income redistribution may have socially or ethically, it cannot be approved on the ground that it stimulates consumption. If, moreover, this postulate is true, those advocating high wage policy and progressive taxation as favorable to economic activity are standing on a shaky foundation. It also follows, however, that those who hold marginal propensities to consume to be equal at all levels of income, are inconsistent if they oppose redistributionist taxation and high wages on the ground that they prevent the saving out of higher incomes necessary to capital accumulation. Certainly if income transfers from high to low incomes do not alter consumption, they can have no effect on saving and the classic argument of the nineteenth century that income concentration is necessary to capital accumulation ceases to have validity in this decade of the twentieth century. As mentioned in footnote 6, however, this argument is of doubtful validity so far as transfers from corporate profits to wages is concerned so long as corporate profits are not paid out as dividends. Applied to the question here at issue, it follows that the diminution of the wage lag by unionism lowered profits below what they might have been with the individual wage bargain, increased demand for consumption somewhat, and was thus inflationary. Since, moreover, this increment of wage income was probably subjected to lower rates than the corporate tax, it also diminished the United States Treasury surplus. Within these limits trade unionism was inflationary in so far as it diminished the wage lag that experience has shown might have existed in a more competitive labor market.

As regards personal income distribution, however, those who hold to the assumption of equi-marginal consumption propensities, are estopped from contending that increased wages are inflationary when they are obtained at the expense of higher income groups. If redis-

taxes applied to low and high incomes. Redistribution from high to low levels of income would increase the total of disposable income, and in the absence of a tax change, would decrease government revenues, all of which is favorable to consumption. In the long run, however, this qualification would not be important because tax policy would have to be adjusted to produce the same revenues and hence to maintain the same level of disposable income.

tribution does not increase consumption, higher labor incomes are neither stimulating in depression nor inflationary in a boom. For policy purposes we must apply this inference impartially. Marginal propensities to consume are equal or unequal independent of the use to which this fact may be put; it makes no difference whether we use it to argue against redistribution on the ground that it does not augment consumption or for redistribution on the ground that it does not diminish savings. We can argue for either, depending on our interests or sentiments. Indeed the only possible position consistent with the postulate of equi-marginal propensities is that the distribution of income is neutral in its effect on prices or economic activity.

The conditions under which income distribution is neutral or unneutral may be classified as follows: (1) Distribution is neutral under both the Keynesian and Classical hypotheses if marginal propensities to consume are equal. (2) Distribution is always neutral, however, under the classical theory regardless of the various propensities to consume because the relations between consumption, saving and investment are so regulated by the rate of interest as to induce full utilization of resources. (3) Under the Keynesian theory this equilibrating function is denied to the rate of interest, but distribution is still neutral so long as new investment outlets are equivalent to the amount the community desires to save, whether large or small. (4) Distribution becomes unneutral under the Keynesian theory only if it results in a desire to save more than the community is willing to invest. (5) Distribution with unequal marginal consumption propensities can be either neutral or unneutral under Keynesian hypotheses, depending upon the amount of saving (ex ante) and investment produced by the particular economic situation. If desired savings are greater than investment, unequal distribution is depressing; if they are equal, it is neutral. If, on the contrary, distribution makes desired savings less than investment, income distribution is inflationary.

IV

During the boom period, investment was more than adequate to offset desired saving. From the evidence showing the pressing demand for both consumption and capital goods in the two years under discussion, we are warranted in denying the relevance of the underconsumptionist doctrine of insufficient demand as well as the opposite, the lack of investment incentives. Consumption and investment combined were more than sufficient fully to utilize all resources at existing prices. Had wages been lower, individual savings would likely have fallen further in the attempt to maintain living standards, and corporations who disbursed only about one-third of profits to stockholders would have had additional funds for plant expansion. This might have induced additional capital formation or smaller borrowings. A greater wage lag, as postulated, would accordingly have resulted neither in depression, as the unions feared, nor in deflation, nor in price stability, but merely in a distribution of income less favorable to labor. With the above qualifications in respect to corporations we may reject the view that trade unionism was responsible for inflation because its monopolistic control over the labor market enabled it to diminish the wage lag that probably would have ensued in a competitive labor market. Substantially the same inflation would have occurred had wages lagged to the same extent as in previous inflationary periods.

Since Keynes we all seem to be too much obsessed with opposing theories of underconsumption, lack of investment incentives, too little or too much saving, optimum consumption-investment relations, excessive profits, and the like, which have little relevance to the recent period when excessive demand from all sources was made possible by a huge money supply. The simpler postulates of classical economics and the quantity theory of money applied with an eye to the lessons of history give us conclusions which, though less profound in terms of more recent economics, are closer to the facts.

To hold trade unions blameless for the inflation may seem to overstate the case, for it seems to be contrary to the fact that by means of strikes and threats of strikes real wages have been jacked up in such industries as coal and cotton textiles. We must not, however, confuse changes in the wage structure with changes in the general wage level. Unskilled and low paid workers seem to have gained relatively to high paid workers. Can we be certain that under conditions of competition sufficient labor could have been obtained in coal mines and in textile mills without these wage increases? May it not be found that the relative plentifulness of unskilled labor is disappearing and the former large pay differentials between skilled and unskilled workers are being narrowed? In each period, prosperity or depression, forces exist which change price relationships, raising some prices and lowering others, and some prices always appear to be "too high," in both prosperity and depression. Relatively to other prices, building costs were high during the depressed 1930's, and they are absolutely and relatively higher today. Yet we find numerous instances in which contractors were hiring building trade workers at rates considerably in excess of union wage scales and finding buyers able and willing to pay for housing at inflated costs. Trade unions may have raised particular prices above competitive levels, but not sufficiently so to raise the whole price level.

In 1919 Keynes condemned the governments of Europe as "reckless in their methods as well as weak" when they sought "to direct on to a class known as 'profiteers' the popular indignation" against inflation. "These 'profiteers,'" he said, "are, broadly speaking, the entrepreneur class of capitalists that is to say, the active and constructive element in the whole capitalist society, who in a period of rapidly rising prices cannot but get rich quick whether they wish it or desire it or not."[7] We have improved on the previous generation by adding labor leaders to our scapegoats, and now have the choice of blaming inflation either on business or labor unions, and we may indulge either propensity with the same justification, that is, substantially none at all.[8]

V

Although trade unionism as a fomenter of inflation does not come off so badly when its results are contrasted with those to be expected in a competitive labor market, that does not end the matter. We must also inquire whether wage policy could have been executed in a manner less conducive to inflation. If popular interest, criticism and acclaim, and the writings of economists and publicists are any criterion for judging opinion, it is widely believed to have been within the power of labor unions either to create or to undo the price movement. It is implied that if unions had stabilized wage rates, refused to ask

[7] J. M. Keynes, *Essays in Persuasion* (London, 1933), p. 78.

[8] During the sixteenth century when prices were constantly rising because of the influx of gold from America, Bishop Latimer (1548) put the blame on "landlordes and rentraisers, step-lordes, unnatural lordes," when it was the landowners who were being expropriated by the rise in prices because of long term leases. In his *An Historical Inquiry into the Production and Consumption of the Precious Metals* (Philadelphia, 1832), William Jacob aptly says: "The bishop was evidently unaware that the influx of gold and silver from the new world was producing a gradual increase of prices, and like other persons in that age sought, with more zeal than judgment, to find the causes of this extraordinary phenomenon. He attributes this, which he treated as a great evil, to enclosures to sheep walks, to regraters, forestallers, and to any cause but the true one, which in his warmth against his neighbours he had totally overlooked, or was unacquainted with" (p. 245). The chief distinction between 1548 and 1948 is that Bishop Latimer expressed these views in his preachments to the King in the service of God and country, whereas we now explain them to Congress to defend pressure groups and vested interests.

for or to accept wage increases and if manufacturers had refused to take additional profits, the price level would have been lower. Such action, it is clear, would not have inhibited others with large cash balances from bidding for goods and raising prices in grey markets. Price stabilization by voluntary action was impossible. It would have required concerted action by the whole society in the form of price and wage control.

What was wanted by the critics of labor was a sacrificial wage policy for the purpose of keeping down prices. This fanciful policy would have reduced demand for food and clothing but it would also have created a large wage lag with the effects already described, and lessened inflation wholly at the expense of organized labor. Unions would have disintegrated or the leadership would have lost control over the membership if they had attempted to carry out such a policy. Why anyone would have expected organized labor to voluntarily follow a sacrificial wage policy, in view of the abandonment of price control, is a problem for social psychology, not economics. Indeed, the implementation of such a policy would have been possible only within the framework of the corporative state.

A sacrificial wage policy would, however, have reduced labor's share of the national income. Salaries, wages and other labor income rose by $17 billions between 1946 and 1948, proprietors and rental income increased by $12 billions in the same period and corporate profits after taxes rose $10 billions, altogether adding up to $39 billions. If labor had had no wage increases, part of the $17 billions additional payroll would have been diverted to other groups and prices would still have risen from the impetus provided by non-labor expenditures, though perhaps not quite so much.

Although the sacrificial wage proposal may seem foolish, we should not cavil at it nor conclude that criticism of unionism has been entirely footless. Admonitions, threats, and other forms of popular exhortation coupled with homilies on "boom and bust" contributed to uncertainty in the public mind, tempered optimism with pessimism, and exerted a braking influence upon the whole community. Public opinion, political threats, and economic opinion biased by its class origin, far from being injurious, had the salutary effect of slowing down the wage and price boom in the administered sectors of the economy and making it possible for wages of white collared workers, to catch up with the trend.[9]

[9] It would, of course, have been better if the federal budget had run a larger surplus and if the Federal Reserve System had been able to prevent the expansion of member bank loans. By the summer of 1948 the preachments of the

We conclude, then, that inflation since the end of price control has probably been smaller in this regimen of administered prices and collective bargaining than it would have been in a society modeled after perfect competition; that the price increase has been no greater and perhaps has been smaller because wages were determined by voluntary collective bargaining rather than by individualistic competition; that a voluntary sacrificial policy would not have stopped inflation and that it is, moreover, an anachronism, impossible of achievement, and not to be expected. It is, however, conceded that the criticism of trade unionism and preachments against inflation probably exerted a favorable psychological effect in diminishing optimism, creating fear of a depression, lowering the stock market, and thus slowing up the inflationary trend.

VI

Let us now turn to the contention that union policies are necessarily inconsistent with full employment at a stable price level. The historical origin of this view is found in the recovery ending in 1937 when wages began to rise rapidly even with many million unemployed, but its present re-emphasis and elucidation can be credited to the psychological impact of the war and postwar experience to which we have just alluded. Our examination of this period did not show that union wage policy may not be inflationary in the future, it merely showed that it had not been so. We have, however, rid ourselves of the misleading and mischievous interpretation that labor has been a driving inflationary force, and thus have cleared the path for a consideration of the incidence of wage policy unbiased by this implicit preconception.

American Bankers Association who had opposed Federal Reserve credit restriction, were creating doubt in the minds of potential borrowers about their solvency, and of bankers about the future value of their loans, causing them to raise standards, diminish the proportions lent on real estate, and otherwise to tighten the credit market. All these things were to the good. It seems unwarranted, therefore, to treat the exhortation process cavalierly as a foolish attempt to persuade individuals to act altruistically contrary to their economic interests. Political and economic exhortation is much like the ecclesiastical where the urge to do the will of God is always accompanied by threats of consequences for disobedience. It is the danger of economic and political reprisal which makes businessmen and labor leaders hesitate to exploit their own interests fully; the fear of future losses which causes bankers to tighten credit even when they still can obtain plentiful reserves. We tend to disparage moral suasion and qualitative controls because we desire more effective quantitative control over money and credit, but this need not make us believe them to be wholly ineffective.

The inflationary influence of unionism is predicated on the basic postulate, assumed to be a categorical *judgment* of fact, that union wage demands will tend to exceed increases in physical productivity. This postulate may be designated as Lewis' Law.[10] For a short time, it is conceivable although not very likely, that higher wages might come out of profits, but this source would soon be dried up and higher wage rates, not offset by increased productivity, would result in higher prices. If the producer could not sell at such prices, unemployment would follow. Wage increases in excess of productivity are therefore inflationary, but still consistent with full employment, if they can be recouped by the producer in higher prices; they are deflationary and will result in unemployment when they cannot be passed on to the consumer. The first condition existed from 1946 to 1948, the second may result whenever the incessant demand for goods abates without a relaxation of higher wage demands.

We have unionism and we desire full employment and stable prices. If the co-existence of all three is impossible, we must choose any combination of two: (1) unionism and full employment (with inflation); (2) unionism and stable prices (without full employment); (3) full employment and stable prices (without unionism). That is the implication of Lewis' Law. Whether the supposed alternatives are in fact actual depends solely on the validity of this law.

The evidential basis for this generalization is found in the in-

---

[10] Although a law is usually named after its discoverer, I have taken the liberty, in this instance, of naming it after its most eminent practitioner, Mr. John L. Lewis, of the United Mine Workers. It should be noticed that this law applies to the general level of wage rates, not to any particular scale.

Many economists have remarked upon this tendency, but only a few will be quoted here. Professor Sumner H. Slichter has said: "Unions are far more likely to force up wages faster than the engineers and managers raise output per man-hour — perhaps 2 per cent or 3 per cent a year faster, perhaps even more. The difference between the rise in money wages and the rise in output per man-hour will have to be compensated by an advance in prices. For example, if output rises by 3 per cent a year and money wages by 5 per cent a year, prices will need to rise by about 2 per cent a year. Otherwise, there will be a creeping increase in unemployment." *Wages and Prices, An Address before the Academy of Political Science* (Columbia University, 1948), pp. 60–61. The same argument is made in his *The American Economy* (New York, Knopf, 1948), pp. 42–45. Professor Gottfried Haberler says: "The powerful trade unions are now in the habit of demanding wage increases of 10 per cent or more per year. Since labor productivity cannot possibly rise at that rate, it follows that prices must rise or unemployment appear. In the long run, union policy will probably be the main obstacle to maintaining a high level of employment for any length of time without a rapidly rising price level." "Causes and Cures of Inflation," *Rev. Econ. Stat.*, Vol. XXX, No. 1 (February 1948), p. 14.

herent desire of workers for higher wages and the widespread belief in their possibility; the increasing strength of unionism; the internal political structure of organized labor requiring leaders to obtain continually wage increases in order to stay in power; and the impossibility of a non-inflationary policy by any single union so long as each union acts independently to advance wages, costs and prices in its industry. Economists now exploring these fields are rediscovering that labor unions act like a nation assuming sovereignty over jobs, and function as a political organization with manifold social, political and organizational aims known to students of labor for half a century. These rediscoveries, though vitiating the naïve assumption that unions operate as the economic man of simplified price theory who was always maximizing something, still need not cause us to doubt that higher wages are and always have been an essential aim of unionism. It follows, accordingly, that if labor could achieve its wishes without opposition from employers or consumers, money wages would rise. If, moreover, a high employment policy is designed to furnish jobs for all at a price set by the union, then it is obvious that the level of wages will be wholly within labor's discretion. This does not, however, end the matter, but rather raises the question whether such a policy is desirable. And if not, whether the aim of full employment necessarily requires that union demands always be acceded to, regardless of price effects. The issue is not whether unions would like higher wages; it is rather whether they will pursue this aim regardless of opposition and whether such opposition must lead to unemployment.

Those who reckon that labor will have its will at all costs are impressed by the growing economic and political power of organized labor, and its determination to use that power to maintain full employment at rising wages.[11] The wage policies growing out of the demands of individual unions, though uncoordinated by design, soon form a national wage pattern and become imbedded in the price system where they remain unless dislodged by some powerful force. Depression is such a force. But it is believed that if depression is avoided, wages will become flexible upward and inflexible downward, and prices likewise will rise during the boom and remain stable in the recession.

[11] The postwar period, however, provides a misleading basis for judging union wage policy. True, the unions continually demanded higher wages, but this action was part of an inflationary movement having more deep-seated causes to which the wage-price spiral was a response. The apparent success of union wage policy was, moreover, deceptive, because of the lag in real wages.

The conjectural generalization which we have branded Lewis' Law does not state an inherent propensity of human beings based on physiological psychology or a behavior pattern of social psychology. Union behavior is not tropismatic, intuitive, habitual or otherwise irrationally invariant heedless of circumstances. High wage demands though deeply ingrained into union custom are modified whenever unions are opposed by forces which are capable of defeating their will. What are these forces?

In a community with a limited money supply, the employer will resist wage increases when they can not be passed on to the consumer and must come out of his profits. While it is true that the abstract danger of inflation will deter no particular union, the concrete fact that the employer can not grant their demands without losing his market and bankrupting himself, will cause unions to take thought. Lewis' Law as a statement of union power is therefore a fiction rather than a fact; a generalization valid only for inflationary periods. We must not think of labor's behavior as following a fixed pattern, but rather as it has already shown itself to be: political in character and adjustable to the hard facts of working, earning, living, and surviving. Labor leaders may act foolishly and at times impetuously, but they will not continually beat their heads against a stone wall. The question remains, therefore, whether the policy of price stability is strong enough to stand against the threats against it, or merely a house of straw which can be blown over with the first puff.

The process of labor union inflation is envisioned as follows: (1) Labor will demand higher wages and threaten a strike. (2) Employers will be forced to grant these requests or to cease operations. (3) They will prefer to raise both wages and prices. (4) Higher prices will require additional bank borrowing, thus increasing the quantity of money. (5) Member banks will lend additional funds if security is ample and if they have excess reserves regardless of the effect on the level of prices. (6) Since credit can only be restricted by Federal Reserve policy, the Federal Reserve System will be forced to choose between preventing inflation or causing unemployment. (7) Faced with these alternatives, it is believed that central banking authorities will always choose the inflationary path or if they should refuse to do so, business and labor will have them replaced by officials who will aid and abet the inflationary trend in the name of full employment.

VII

Inflation induced by organized labor must have its matrix in full employment; but full employment could arise from two sources: private demand for consumption and investment, or from governmental spending. In the first case, bank credits will be given to private industry, and in the second, to the government, but in both the net effect will be an expansion of the volume of bank deposits. Implicit in the fear of business inflation is the assumption that private aggregate demand will be sufficient to promote full employment if left unhindered by restrictive banking policy. Credit expansion will come via the classical route of business borrowing, and bank assets will increasingly take the form of business loans. Under these circumstances, the banks will be in a position to thwart prosperity and inflation by refusing to grant inflationary credits, but they will not be needed to promote it.

The fear of inflation also arises from the belief that full employment and stable prices are just as inconsistent with a privately produced prosperity as with a governmentally induced full-employment program, wage policy being the same in either case. In the event of a depression, wages will remain rigid. Then as unemployment grows, public works will replace private demand and full employment will return. Even before the level of output and employment reaches a maximum, labor will again demand higher wages which will be granted by increasing the public debt and manufacturing new credits. Prices will then rise further until the next depression, when the process will again be repeated. It can be pointed out that wages and prices rose at an increasing rate just preceding the 1937 depression even while many million men were still unemployed, and Professor Slichter has shown that it took a rapidly increasing level of expenditure to produce additional output during the war period. This is, of course, the barrier that Keynes envisioned when he showed that full employment could be reached without inflation only if output was fully elastic until full employment was reached, after which increasing expenditure would merely raise prices.

This inflationary tendency created by labor policy would be present in both types of full employment and must be further distinguished from other cost-raising physical and economic factors operating independent of labor policy such as bottlenecks, material scarcities, laxness of labor and management, and rising real costs due to insufficient capacity for a full-employment economy.[12] With business

[12] Rising real costs in short-run cyclical fluctuations are probably less likely

inflation, labor will be striking against the individual employer and exerting pressure for credit expansion on the Federal Reserve System; in the case of government spending, labor would have to put political pressure on Congress to increase the size of the deficit. In the former case it seems doubtful that labor can be successful in causing a price rise so long as the money supply is not excessive. Except in periods of high demand, labor is continuously beset by fears of unemployment. Business inflations, moreover, instead of being inaugurated by wage demands, come from optimistic expectations and bank borrowings which raise prices ahead of wages. The need for additional credits to pay higher wages has not, and is not likely to become the initiating force in credit expansion because no individual producer can act on the assumption that his own market will be expanded by an increase in his own payrolls. It seems unlikely, therefore, that labor can alter the traditional wage lag into a wage lead.

Although attempts of individual unions to keep their wages "in line" with others brings some semblance of a national wage policy, still their actions are not concerted enough to produce a general inflationary trend. Labor is not organized as yet into one big union making national agreements affecting all workers, and even if this were true, factory payrolls would still not be the only source of demand for goods. Producers could not simply grant increased wages, raise prices, and then ask the banks to finance such a policy; they would still need to worry about pricing themselves out of the market.

If inflation threatens, in spite of all these obstacles, it is still the function of the central bank to make it apparent that the necessary credits to sustain it will not be forthcoming. Such a monetary policy will increase employer resistance, weaken the market for goods, and lessen the will to strike. It is not by raising the cost of credit, but by threatening to curtail its amount, at any cost if necessary, that the central bank exerts pressure against rising wage and price levels.

VIII

The belief that organized labor can control the price level derives to a large degree also from the conception of trade unions as monopolists. We should therefore examine the nature and extent of labor monopoly as it bears on credit and price policy.

Labor monopoly is intrinsically different, and also less powerful

than constant costs, except where capacity is insufficient. See Alvin H. Hansen, "Cost Functions and Full Employment," *Am. Econ. Rev.*, Vol. XXXVII, No. 4 (September 1947), p. 552.

than monopoly exercised by business firms. According to the theory of monopoly, the producer of any product has monopoly power when he can raise his price without losing all of his market. He can vary production by small increments according to its effect on costs and revenue so as to yield the highest net profit. He does not lose his entire market if he raises his price as he would under perfect competition. Labor, on the other hand, bargains for all members of the union; in striking for a 5 per cent wage increase it must be willing to sacrifice not an increment of employment and income, but all employment and income for the duration of the strike. Even the most powerful union is in the same theoretical position as a seller under perfect competition, who must sell at the market price or not at all. The loss to the worker is the total value of his labor for the period of the strike, plus the possible loss of employment after he wins the strike in so far as he has priced himself out of the market; the loss of the employer is not his total product but only his fixed costs and possible profit. No producer monopolist operates on the all-or-none basis — he need not risk selling no goods at all if he raises his price by a few per cent. Yet this is labor's predicament in a strike. It is, therefore, misleading to think of labor union monopoly power, based as it is on the small resources of its members and the pitifully small power to resist long unemployment without suffering and starvation, as equal to the power of industrial monopoly, backed by huge financial resources and able to sustain losses for a long period of time without impairing its financial health and stability.

But let us grant for the sake of analysis that the unions can overcome the resistance of the employer and that he seeks to obtain additional funds to finance a higher wage bill. Where is he to get them? When his profit margin is seriously impaired, earnings will be low and the stock and the bond markets will be closed to him. If he seeks to borrow from the banks, they will be doubtful about financing him. But supposing that he overcomes these disabilities and is still able to make a financial showing, the banks can loan only if they have excess reserves which under normal conditions are subject to central banking control. To be successful then in their assumed policy, labor unions must also control banking policy.

IX

The Board of Governors of the Federal Reserve System by predilection, previous training, experience and personal association are not likely to give extraordinary weight to a policy promoted by labor leaders, particularly when in doing so they would need go counter to other elements in the community and to the historical function and traditions of central bankers.

Since the war they have failed to restrict credit only because they felt it a paramount duty to maintain the government bond market. It is true that in the past credit has not been readily curtailed when the initiative to credit expansion came from the profit expectations of business and when such curtailment augured depression. Prevention of inflation is, however, now an established national policy accepted by workers even more so than by farmers and other elements of the population, and it seems quite unlikely that labor leaders would try to force inflation upon the Federal Reserve System.[13]

Once inflation gets under way, it creates interests favorable to its continuance and it is therefore the duty of central banks to maintain such stability that these interests will not have a chance to become powerful. That central bankers find opposition to these policies is not novel. Throughout the history of central banking, the monetary authority has always met with resistance when it sought to stop inflation by credit restriction. Those committed to higher prices for commodities, real estate and securities will oppose a restrictionist policy; business firms selling on credit will find their sales curtailed, commercial bankers seeking profits through further loan expansion may view it as an interference with their operations, merchants who might be thrown into bankruptcy by a price decline, speculators, brokers and wholesalers who have large commitments on narrow margins, will urge that the inflation be carried on just a bit further, until they presumably will be able to unload. Promoters of new enterprises, security dealers heavily extended on new flotations, real estate speculators — all will condemn a policy which will cause heavy loss. Farmers hoping to unload crops at rising prices will see in it a plot

[13] Price stabilization is, however, not an absolute end to be pursued under all circumstances. A general rise in prices is not always monetary in origin; it may be due either to an abundance of money or to a scarcity of goods. It has never been considered to be within the province of a central bank to prevent a price rise originating in a general crop failure or a breakdown of production such as happened in Europe at the end of the war. The rise in agricultural prices in this country during 1946 and 1947 resulted from small crops and intense domestic and foreign need for food. It could have been prevented only by a policy which would have created a mass of unemployed who were unable to buy food. In such circumstances, monetary policy should not be used to maintain a stable price level. In this as in other matters of economic policy, the remedy for a situation must depend upon correct analysis of its causes; banks can contain inflation only in so far as it is caused by the money supply.

to deprive them of their income. In the history of this country, land speculators cursed the specie circular which burst their bubble in 1837, farmers and railroad interests among others fought the resumption of specie payments and favored free silver and greenbackism. Since the Federal Reserve System was inaugurated it has been criticized for every major credit restriction: W. G. P. Harding was driven off the Federal Reserve Board because of the myth that the Federal Reserve had conspired to deflate the farmer in 1920; in 1925 easy money created to help put Britain on the gold standard aided a stock market inflation which had many protagonists until the break in 1929, a slight tightening of credit in 1937 called forth wide criticisms, and even in the great inflation of 1946–1948, bankers, industrialists, veterans and many other patriots were averse to credit restriction.

A contraction of credit, or even a failure to expand, will create trouble for those speculating for a rise, but this is a risk which must be taken. "A crisis," says Mr. R. G. Hawtrey, "may be regarded as a struggle to maintain the standard of value."[14] We can avoid the crisis by giving up the struggle and going the way of inflation, or we can face the crisis and maintain the standard of value. Central bankers must be willing to act courageously regardless of the pressures which are put upon them. We have destroyed the tabu of the gold standard which the masses of people had accepted without question as a justification for preserving the value of money, but we have not put price stability in its place. Instead, we have set up full employment as a symbol to be worshipped without realizing the sacrifices that unreasoning obedience to it might demand.

Faced with this situation, some hold that we should accept a gradually rising price level as a necessary consequence of trade unionism and full-employment policy and sacrifice the fixed-income group and creditor classes. Others suggest that fixed-income groups be abolished by making all bonds, pensions, and annuities subject to changes in the price level. All such proposals are, however, self-defeating, for if all incomes moved up together the advantage of inflation to any single group would be nil and those seeking to gain at the expense of the rest would devise other means of benefiting by price changes. The objection to inflation is its unequal incidence.

The proposal of a gradually rising price level as a deliberate national policy is, moreover, self-contradictory. Beginning in the 16th century it was possible for prices to rise over a period of 150 years as gold came into Europe from the new world. A gradual rise in

[14] *Currency and Credit* (London, 1923), p. 156.

prices was also possible when changes in the gold and silver supply or even in bank credit were the product of unconscious forces and were neither forecast nor deliberately planned. In a modern paper money regime, any planned inflation will be immediately discounted. If a government deliberately plans that prices will be 10 per cent higher at the end of every year than at the beginning, the anticipated price rise will be discounted at once by holders of goods and securities. They will immediately raise prices to the discounted future value and refuse to sell except at this price. It will then be found necessary to permit prices to rise at once by making more money available, and then to permit even further inflation, or to lose the purported stimulation of a gradually rising price level. In brief, a planned gradual rise in the price level is self-contradictory because it will be discounted if it is generally known, and under modern conditions, if it is planned, it will be known.[15] The policy of a planned gradually rising price level is simply a chimera arising out of defeatism, confusion, and despair. It is compounded out of an erroneous comparison with an unplanned rise in prices, an oversimplified theory of employment, a fear of vested interests, and disillusion over the possibility of rational economic, fiscal, and monetary policy.

A policy of high employment at a stable level of prices is, on the other hand, both rational and possible. Once we are committed

[15] The discounting of expectations assumes that the public acts with a reasonable amount of knowledge and intelligence which I think may be granted in this case. It also assumes that planning certain enough to be stimulating is certain enough to be discounted. Another view is, of course, possible, namely that businessmen knowing that prices are going to rise will still act as if they are remaining stable and will not discount their expectations. The latter view is taken by Thorstein Veblen: "The Federal Reserve . . . inflates the businessmen's expectations of gain, and thereby speeds up business and industry; for among the securely known facts of psychology, as touches the conduct of business, is the ingrained persuasion that the money unit is stable; (This persuasion is known not to accord with fact, but still it remains a principle of conduct. It has something like an instinctive force; or perhaps rather, it is something like a tropismatic reaction, in that the presumption is acted on even when it is known to be misleading) the value of the money unit being the base-line of business transactions. Therefore, an inflation of prices is rated as an accession of wealth. Therefore such an inflation will impart confidence and buoyancy and raise great expectations, by a tropismatic stimulation of the businessmen's sensibilities if not by logical inference; and logic is after all a feeble defense in the face of a tropismatic stimulation, as is abundantly shown by the history of business cycles." *Absentee Ownership* (New York, 1923), p. 179. Far from believing that inflation would promote full employment, Veblen showed that it was followed by a "breakdown, a slaughter of the innocents, called a period of liquidation" (p. 180).

to such a policy, no group can hope to improve its share of the national income by means of policies leading to inflation. If any group forges recklessly ahead with such wage and price policies, it will be brought to a halt by its own folly until its policies are adjusted to the national interest. The central bank will resist inflationism and labor and business will be obliged to act accordingly. Such resistance may provoke an immediate downturn in business but the alternative of continued inflation is worse. The guaranty of opportunity by society cannot be unconditional; it requires that individuals and groups act so as to make this end possible of fulfillment. If they can not do so, then one end or the other must be sacrificed, and in the long run it would be better to sacrifice that of full employment. To sacrifice price stability will ultimately destroy the currency and create unemployment and the loss of social and economic stability. We can conclude, however, on the hopeful note that despite many contentions to the contrary, there is in the war experience and in the present structure of our society little evidence that labor has either the determination or the power to destroy price stability, social order and the life of other groups by pursuing a policy of inflationism regardless of its economic and social consequences.

X

Let us now turn to fiscally induced inflation. Although the Employment Act of 1946 does not promise full employment by means of fiscal policy, we may ask how trade unionism would impinge upon such a policy should it be adopted. If full employment is insured by governmental spending regardless of its effect on costs and prices, we may feel reasonably sure that labor will make little effort to keep its wage rates in line so as not to price itself out of the market. Producers, knowing that government will take whatever goods they produce regardless of price (as in the cost-plus contracts during the war) will have no need to resist wage demands and unions will have no hesitancy in making them. If, for example, building costs rise too high for the incomes of prospective buyers and unemployment ensues in this trade, it would seem that the industry ought to reduce its costs.[16] Should government, however, assure the industry that it will provide orders whenever private business slumps, the incentive to price its product for private demand will disappear. Wages, costs and prices

[16] This is in fact the position taken by President Truman in his *Report to Congress, January, 1949.*

will rise and never slump. The error in attempting to insure full employment by the simple device of compensatory spending is that it removes all incentives for producers to adjust their costs to the private market; it assures demand for the entire national product without reference to quality and price, and provides a seller's market for goods and services at a price fixed by the sellers. To describe this guaranty is enough to condemn it.

When the Employment Act of 1946 was under consideration, it was suggested that compensatory policies should be followed only in so far as they were consistent with a stable cost of living, but no such provision was included in the act. If, therefore, we should get inflation by the route of compensatory spending under a full-employment policy, it will not be because of trade unionism alone, but because in a seller's market every element in the community would be induced to raise prices and never to lower them. The principles of functional finance sometimes seem to imply that compensatory devices be used regardless of the cause of unemployment. In some circles, compensatory finance has become a dogma of economic policy with the same authority for its votaries as the "invisible hand" of Adam Smith had for the laissez-faire school, Say's Law for the neoclassicists, and surplus value for the Marxians. As a dogma, it overlooks the multiple causes of depression and forgets that the cure of unemployment must depend upon its cause. If the cause be unbalanced price relationships, such as excessive prices for houses, automobiles, etc., then the remedy is to reduce these prices, not to guarantee a market for the products of these industries at inflated levels. If the cause be underconsumption in the Hobsonian sense, then the remedy is to change the distribution of income; if the cause be inadequate investment incentives, these will need to be augmented. We conclude, then, that inflation will result from cyclical depression or stagnation only if government guarantees full employment regardless of its effect on costs or prices and pursues an inflationary policy to achieve it. Neither labor nor the central bank can prevent the consequences of such a policy; it can be prevented only by ridding ourselves of the dogmas responsible for it.

If we recognize that compensatory finance is not the sole means of maintaining aggregate demand in a free market-profit economy, we should not encourage the various economic groups in the belief that they will be protected from the consequences of their own folly by government spending. We should rather make them see the necessity of adjusting their own prices and policies so as to create a demand for their own product. It may be necessary to declare quite deliberately that government will refuse to maintain effective demand in those sectors which refuse to adjust their costs and prices to private market demand, and to use compensatory finance only when the fault does not lie in wage-price policies. Compensatory policies which look only to the aggregates of consumption and investment will create expectation for further inflation and hardly any inducement to correct basic causes of underemployment. In so far as the Keynesian Revolution has come to this, it is a purely inflationary philosophy which must end in disaster. But it need not be so. We can still take into account aggregative relations between income, consumption, savings and investment as emphasized by Malthus, Hobson, Keynes and by the underconsumptionists, without ignoring the fact that equilibrium is also conditioned by the relations between wages, costs, and prices as described by the classical tradition.

Keynes created a false disjunction between classical and aggregate equilibrium which has produced a fateful dichotomy between policies designed to promote balanced price relationships and those aimed at balanced income relationships. We need not reject the classical cost-price balance in order to accept the Keynesian savings-investment equilibrium; we can rather accept the more reasonable conclusion that both the system of individual prices and the aggregates need to be in an optimum relationship in order to bring about full utilization of resources.

The two systems are indeed not contradictory but complimentary. The truth in the classical system was its emphasis upon the need for workable relationships between individual prices to facilitate full employment; the error was the view that the rate of interest produced full employment automatically. The truth in the Keynesian system was in its emphasis upon the need for workable relationships between the aggregates of income, consumption, savings and investment which it showed were not produced automatically by the rate of interest; the error was that it assumed these aggregates could be brought into optimum relationships by manipulating the rate of interest, the quantity of money, the distribution of income, and the fiscal policy of governments. It is not necessary to accept these exclusive alternatives, and if it is not necessary, it is not desirable. To accept without modification the classical view is to ignore the aggregative relations which were emphasized by Malthus, Marx, Hobson and others before and after Keynes; to accept the compensatory view without modification is to embark upon a policy which neglects the need for incentives to adjust relative prices to market demand.

We conclude, therefore, that governmentally induced inflation must result from fiscal policy only if it is pursued without regard to the cause of underemployment; and that such a monolithic policy should be cast aside for one that is free from dogma, though not from error in comprehension and execution, but more comprehensive and hence likely to be more timely and fruitful.

XI

If the foregoing is essentially correct, we need not worry about the dire forebodings of those who deny the compatibility of trade unionism with the objectives of high employment and stable prices. We need not set out to disorganize our social life by a war on organized labor; nor let inflation rob the creditor class, the fixed-income groups, and those who have saved for old age; nor mournfully consign part of our resources to idleness and condemn our people to the humiliation and despair of large-scale unemployment. The view posing these stark alternatives, though it flows cogently from its postulates and is not without some truth, still is insufficiently factually accurate for purposes of national policy. We can, moreover, continue our efforts to maintain the high standard of living and the opportunity which full employment makes possible, without inaugurating controls over individual prices and wages.

If we do not need to destroy unionism in order to preserve price stability, neither do we need to establish, as has been sometimes suggested, a board to formulate and enforce a national wage policy fixing the general level of wages. In any event, such a board would hardly be effectual, for, if organized labor were powerful enough to force its views upon employers, bankers, and a reluctant Federal Reserve Board, it would most likely also be able to have its way with a national labor board. A Federal Reserve Board seeking to maintain sound economic conditions for the whole community does not aim its measures at any particular group such as a wage board would have to do, and in pursuit of these wider social aims, it could more easily resist the demands of any one group than could a special board set up for their specific control. Quite likely, a national wage board would be heavily weighted with labor members or public members acceptable to labor who would follow the traditional policy of accepting compromise wage increases, and resisting cuts. It is hard to visualize such a board, no matter how cogent its arguments and eloquent its expression, uncompromisingly resisting wage demands which were within its power to grant. Credit policy, on the other hand, being aimed at the control of total monetary demand leaves its allocation to the market which in turn dominates wage negotiations. An employer, resisting wage demands because the market will not stand them, is in a much stronger position to stop an inflationary rise than a wage board, which apparently has no direct financial responsibility for the result. We may, therefore, tentatively conclude that the establishment of a board to set a national wage pattern would probably be more inflationary than otherwise, and if, moreover, wages were subject to control, so would prices have to be, and we would end up in the position envisioned by those who believe that full employment is impossible without complete regimentation.

Under the circumstances, it seems wiser to continue over-all control of effective demand and to leave the rest of the economy free to adjust individual prices and wages to the resulting market. The concept of an unlimited monetary demand is, of course, inconsistent with price stability; it is this concept of which we must rid ourselves, not of trade unionism. If, however, it be found desirable to restrict, regulate or destroy monopoly, whether of business, agriculture or labor because of its effect on prices and production, that can still be done for its own sake; it need not be done in order to control the general price level. The same holds true relative to the need of rules to prevent work stoppages which may paralyze the nation or be dangerous to health and safety. The war and postwar experiences which engendered the ideas of direct controls over prices and wages are not typical of a peacetime economy because war demand is unlimited whereas in peace the consumer can withhold purchases until prices are in line with this income. The present mixture of monopoly, unionism and competition will not operate after the model of perfect competition. We must accordingly learn to live by the more complex rules of a collective bargaining economy, but we need not yet admit that desiderata of stability and prosperity make our ultimate choice one between perfect competition and complete regimentation. These alternatives have a plausible validity so long as we do not examine too closely the reality of the postulates on which they rest, and, like much abstract theory of this type, present us with apparent alternatives true only at the limits. In a dynamic life, social adjustments, though following no fixed pattern, can be made between the extremes according to the strength of conflicting forces. This is the aim of a collective-bargaining economy with individuals who are still exposed to losses and gains as members of their group and therefore provided with strong incentives to act intelligently in their own and in the social interest.

PART TWO

TWO VIEWS OF THE COST–PUSH ARGUMENT

CHARLES SCHULTZE

Recent Inflation
in the United States*

In the following brief excerpt Schultze summarizes what he believes to be the causes of the creeping inflation of the 1950's. In effect, Schultze's theory is a variant of the cost-push argument. In his Chart 3 he shows that industries which experience a 4 percent increase in output (the assumed increase in supply resulting from productivity gains) still show substantial price increases, presumably because of cost-push elements.

* Reprinted from Joint Economic Committee, Study Paper No. 1 (Washington, 1959), pp. 73–77.

32

Although Schultze considers sectoral shifts in demand as the initiating element in the inflation process, it does not appear from his graph that sectoral shifts are a necessary condition for inflation. If all industries shared equally in the hypothetical national growth in productivity, and if aggregate demand were sufficiently strong to maintain full employment, the graph would describe a situation of general price increases.

It may be that during the two-year boom period from mid-1955 to mid-1957 demand shifts were indeed instrumental in setting cost-push inflation in motion. During this period there was a distinct shift in relative demand toward capital goods (the period is usually referred to as one of investment boom). Thus, according to the Schultze theory, although there were only minor changes in aggregate demand (total output), the investment sector, in response to increased demand for capital goods, experienced price increases. Meanwhile prices fell but slightly, remained steady, or even rose slightly within the declining consumer sector, depending on the relative position of different industries, as the deflationary pressure in this sector was restrained by the ratchet effect of administered prices and wages.

It might be argued, however, that shifts in demand are continually taking place. Therefore, if Schultze's theory applies, the inflationary impact of these shifts is always with us. Nevertheless, except for the brief two-year period in question, there has never been a significant price rise in the United States not associated with war-stimulated excess demand, other than the customary reflation of prices following depression bottoms. Schultze argues that the demand shift must be sharp to be felt on the general price level, and concludes that in any case the total effect of this type of inflation is slight. Perhaps this demand-shift cost-push conjunction is so rare a phenomenon as to explain why it has occurred but once in our economic experience. But there have been frequent historical instances of internal shifts in demand coupled with relatively constant total output, so that one is puzzled at the failure of prices to rise in these numerous episodes.

There is an argument for the demand-shift inflationary thesis without recourse to the *deus ex machina* of a "floor" set by wage-price rigidities. If demand shifts from a sector of high and relatively increasing productivity to a sector of low and relatively declining productivity, then on balance the effect of the shift is inflationary. What would result from these conditions would be the inflationary effects of a decline in average national productivity. Just such shifts have occurred. On balance demand has shifted from goods (high and rising productivity) to services (low and relatively declining productivity). There is no evidence that the effects of this shift have been strong enough to cause inflation by their own power. In fact, average productivity has been rising steadily despite this shift, so that whatever inflationary aspects are associated with the shift have been swamped by more powerful influences on prices. Nevertheless, as an isolated force this shift has added to the weight of inflationary elements.

The same type of reasoning could be applied to Schultze's theory. Demand shift is a weak independent inflationary element. Operating in isolation it would act to increase prices; but only rarely, in fact just once, have the other numerous and stronger influences on prices been in such a condition of equilibrium as to permit the slight inflationary aspects of demand shift to be felt.

OUR explanation of creeping inflation rests on a combination of factors. It originates in the general excess demands which temporarily emerge as we pass from recession to full employment, and from the particularized excess demands which often remain when the aggregate excess has been eliminated. But it is perpetuated and spread throughout the economy by the downward rigidities and cost-oriented nature of our price and wage making institutions.

THE RELATIONSHIP OF RELATIVE DEMANDS TO RELATIVE PRICES

If the hypothesis we have presented is substantially correct we should find that the relative rise in prices among different commodities is related to the relative strength of demand, *but* with an upward bias. A given increase in demand will lead to a price increase significantly larger than the price decline accompanying a fall in demand of the same magnitude. This result emerges from the existence of downward rigidities in prices and from the influence on prices of cost increases generated in areas of rising demands.

We have no measures of excess demand. However, we can use the relative rates of growth in output as a rough and ready substitute. A growing labor force and rising productivity imply a constantly increasing level of full employment output; supply curves are continually shifting and to the right. If prices and wages were perfectly flexible, price increases would only be associated with increases in output larger than the rightward shift in supply curves. Schematically, the situation is depicted below in Chart I.

CHART I

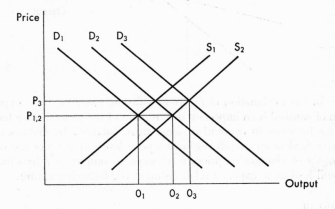

As the supply curve shifts rightward demand does not become excess, and prices do not rise, unless demand increases by a larger amount than supply. A plot of price changes against output changes industry by industry during some given period, say a year, should produce a relationship about like that shown in Chart II. If aggregate demand is not excessive, then aggregate output can rise moderately with no increase in the average level of prices. For illustrative purposes we have assumed a 4 per cent rightward shift in supply curves. Prices should fall in industries whose output gain is less than average, while industries with larger than average output gains will experience price increases. If resources are very mobile, then a significant dispersion in the mix of demand should yield a price-output curve like B above — relative prices need change only modestly to reallocate resources. If resources are immobile, larger than average output gains will generally require substantial price increases, and declining output will involve large price decreases — curve A.[1]

CHART II

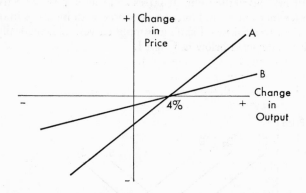

In our explanation of creeping inflation, however, the composition of demand is an important determinant of the general price level. Sharp increases in demand in some areas, balanced by decreases in others, lead to an overall rise in the price level. If we plot the relationship of changes in prices to changes in output, our hypothesis would lead us to expect a relationship of the following nature:

CHART III

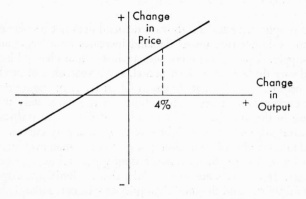

[1] The greater the mobility of resources the more elastic will be the supply curves of Chart II.

There will be an upward bias in the relationship of prices to demand. Industries with no excess demands — under our rough assumptions, those whose output is expanding modestly — will nevertheless be characterized by rising prices. Only those industries with substantial deficiencies of demand will be marked by falling prices. *If we match, in some detail, changes in industrial prices and output during the 1955–57 period we find a relationship exactly as depicted above.* There was a positive association between price increases and output increases; but the relationship is not the one that would exist if prices and wages were symmetrically flexible. Although the average gain in output was quite small, there was a significant rise in the general price level. Many industries whose output rise was significantly less than the rightward shift in their supply curves nevertheless raised their prices. Generally speaking, prices were reduced only in situations where production was sharply curtailed.

A demonstration that price increases tend to be associated with demand increases, industry by industry, is, therefore, no proof that inflation is generated solely by excess aggregate demand. The mere fact of such a relationship is quite consistent with the hypothesis we have presented in this chapter. Indeed the specific shape of the relationship and the values of its parameters during recent years tend to confirm the fact that the inflation was not primarily generated by excess aggregate demand.

SECULAR INFLATION

The mechanism by which shifts in the composition of demand tend to generate a rising price level did not suddenly emerge in the postwar period. Many prices and most wages have always been relatively insensitive to moderate downward shifts in demand. The magnetic effect of rising costs in particular sectors of the economy on the general level of costs is not a novel phenomenon. But the recurrence of sharp and prolonged general depressions was usually sufficient to break through these rigidities and enforce a reduction in the most insensitive prices and wages.

During depression years the widespread bankruptcies and reorganizations also led to massive write-downs in the value of fixed assets. This provided an additional damper on secularly rising prices. Increases in capital goods prices which accompany a short run inflation normally leave a legacy of continued upward pressure on the level of costs. Even after capital goods prices cease to rise the replacement of lower priced assets — valued at the prices ruling before the inflation began — with new, higher priced assets tends to raise the level of costs. The fact that the new capital goods are more efficient than the ones they replace is no offset, for the rise in productivity so generated will normally be absorbed by higher returns to factors of production. One may argue over the importance of capital costs per unit in short-run pricing decisions. In the long run it is quite clear that they do affect prices. The downward revaluations of capital assets during severe depressions removed this legacy of rising capital costs left by prior inflations. Thus by breaking through the ratchet which holds up prices and costs, the severe depressions of earlier periods interrupted the tendency of prices and wages to rise secularly. There is little likelihood that any administration would permit a recurrence of such protracted depressions in the future.

There is yet another way in which downward rigidities in the price system tend to engender a secular rise in the price level. We pointed out earlier that productivity increases most rapidly during the early phases of a recovery as the fruits of earlier investment outlays are realized. Even though wages increase moderately during such periods, profit margins rise dramatically. Prices, based on the level of costs incurred during the prior boom, are too high relative to the new and lower level of costs. Had prices been reduced during the recession, profit margins would simply return to a normal level during recovery. Downward price rigidity, however, implies excessively high margins when recovery occurs. *Ex ante profit margins,* at a full employment level of output are too high in the recession, even though ex post margins are somewhat lower than normal. The excessive margins lead in turn to overexuberant expectations when the economy moves back to full employment. As a consequence, even though prices of final goods do not rise during the typical recovery, factor prices are bid up. We have the kind of process emphasized by Hansen and Turvey — a factor price inflation. The sharp rise in profit margins is halted, and then reversed well before the succeeding downturn in economic activity.

If prices were flexible during recession, the rapid growth in productivity during the subsequent recovery would restore margins to normal levels, with costs somewhat lower than at the prior peak. The sharp productivity advances in recovery years would thus provide an offset to the rise in costs and prices during other periods. Instead, with rigid commodity prices, the productivity gains are dissipated in higher factor prices.

The rigidities in costs and prices are thus sufficient to provide a ratchet under the price level, preventing its falling back from levels attained during periods of inflation. Adjustments in relative prices tend to be accomplished by upward movements only, even though aggregate demand is not excessive. Imbalances in general price-wage relationships also tend to be overcome by a rise in one relative to the other, rather than by a mutual adjustment toward a common center.

SOME QUALIFYING COMMENTS

The kind of inflation which results from the process we have described in this chapter is a gradual process. So long as aggregate demand is not excessive, inflation will be mild. The rigidities and cost-oriented characteristics of prices and wages are not so firm that they completely withstand the influence of deficient demand. Our exclusive concentration on the inflationary consequences of sharp changes in the composition of demand should not be interpreted as a sign that the resulting inflation is a particularly awesome affair. Popular articles on inflation often begin by reciting all of the evils of a hyperinflation, and then assign those evils as the consequence of any inflation, no matter how gradual. The inflation we have here described need have none of these characteristics. Mild inflation is, in fact, one of the ways in which an economy with downward rigidities in its cost and price structure allocates resources. There are arbitrary income gains and losses accompanying any shifting about of resources. Whether individual well-being and social equity are better preserved when resource shifts entail only relative price changes instead of overall price increases I do not pretend to know. Certainly, however, it is not a question whose answer is obvious.

GARDNER ACKLEY

A Third Approach to the Analysis and Control of Inflation*

Most exponents of cost-push theory assume that the sequence of increased wages and prices would be accompanied by unemployment. Thus, the presence of or growth in unemployment during a period of rising prices would serve as an indicator of cost-push elements in

* Reprinted from Joint Economic Committee, *The Relationship of Prices to Economic Stability and Growth* (Washington, D. C., 1958), pp. 619–636.

the inflationary process. Ackley takes a macroeconomic approach in his review of the nature of cost-push inflation. From this viewpoint, unemployment does not automatically follow a general wage increase. With unchanging aggregate demand, prices tend to rise from the wage push in proportion to the increase in wages.

The main guide, then, to the difference between cost-push and demand-pull inflation—the presence of unemployment when cost-push factors are operating—would often be missing. It would follow then that if prices rose under conditions of low unemployment, either the cost-push or the demand-pull element could be the dominant causal factor since cost push is also consistent with full employment. If prices rose gradually when unemployment was high and the economy weak, the situation would fit only the cost-push theory. But Ackley's discussion of economic "frictions" and the practical impossibility of achieving full employment show that even the period of "creeping inflation" might be considered one of reasonably low unemployment.

Ackley's main contribution in comparing demand pull with cost push is certainly not to deny that cost-push elements have ever dominated. It is quite the opposite. He points out that during periods of high employment, save for the super-boom post World War II and Korean War periods, in theory either cost-push or demand-pull factors, or both, could have prevailed, and in practice it would be almost impossible to assign the prime responsibility to either for inflation.

Certainly Ackley's emphasis on the subjective character of numerous firms' pricing policies has restored the imbalance in cost-push analysis. Theories that conceive of wages set in an administered manner and prices by the impersonal forces of the market place must by definition consider only wage increases as cost-push elements. However, once it is acknowledged that many prices, especially the pattern-setting ones of the major industries, are also established by conscious decisions rather than by passive acquiescence to market forces, the responsibility for cost-push inflation may rest on management just as much as on labor.

Despite the prevalence of mark-up, or cost-plus, pricing—and there is no evidence to deny Ackley's contention that most prices and wages are set in this manner—the mark-up theory of inflation suffers from more shortcomings than Ackley specifies. These deficiencies appear both in the description of the origins of an inflation and its continuation.

While Ackley's point that inflation theories overstress the initial causes of an inflation, rather than carefully analyze the reasons for its continuation, is well taken, it is still important to learn what sets an inflationary process in motion. According to the mark-up theory, since wages and prices are set subjectively, all beginnings of inflation are of the cost-push type. However, if the antecedents of these management and union pricing decisions are considered, then the actual origin of an inflation can fit either the cost-push or demand-pull doctrine. If the decision to raise the price of a product or a factor of production results from demand pressure in either the product or labor market, then mark-up pricing becomes the instrument of demand-pull inflation. On the other hand, if inflation is generated by a subjective change in mark-ups unprompted by external market pressures, the resulting inflation can be considered as of the cost-push type.

The mark-up theory is weakest in its description of the continuation process of an inflation. According to the theory, the inflation, once started, would continue indefinitely. Ackley acknowledges that improvements in productive efficiency might put a brake on inflation but notes that if management as well as labor attempts to appropriate productivity gains, the gains will not retard the inflationary spiral. But we know that inflations do run their courses and prices do enjoy long periods of stability. To explain the end of the inflation, we must again look to a weakening of market pressure as unemployment rises and sales fall in response to price and wage increases (removal of demand-pull elements); or we must look to an autonomous reduction in required mark-ups (elimination of cost-push elements). In either case, mark-up pricing of goods and factors serves as an instrument of inflation and not as an independent force.

PRICE LEVEL AND PRICE STRUCTURE

As many contributors to this compendium have no doubt stressed, the "problem" of prices has a dual aspect: Structure and level. By their internal structure — the relationship of each price to all others — prices (including wage rates) influence the allocation of productive activity, and the distribution of income, among products or industries, among various geographical regions, and among the various types of suppliers of productive services. In the analysis of these problems, the concern is always with relative prices — wage rates and other cost prices relative to selling prices; price of product A compared to prices of products B, C, and D; wage rates in city W versus those in cities X, Y, and Z; the prices that determine consumer incomes compared with the prices that consumers must pay; the prices of capital goods relative to those of end products; and so on.

This problem of price structure can at least conceptually be separated from that of price level. For the level can change without the structure changing, and the structure can alter leaving the average level in some sense unchanged.[1]

I intend to focus my discussion primarily on the aspect of price level and — since that is our real problem — on the avoidance of inflation. The basic approach that I shall develop is full of implications about the functioning of relative prices in their roles as allocators of resources; but I shall not attempt to develop these implications here.

Economists have come to distinguish two general kinds of inflation. They are really only pure or ideal types. But we often imply that these polar types actually occur in nearly pure form in the real world; indeed, one gets the impression that all actual inflations are either of the one kind or the other. These two kinds are usually called demand inflation on the one hand, and cost inflation on the other.[2]

I intend to review briefly the more-or-less accepted analyses of these two types of inflation. But I shall then indicate why I find the distinction both unrealistic and, to some extent, even logically invalid. I shall suggest a third analysis which, although it incorporates elements from the first two, provides what I think is a superior framework for the analysis of the problem of inflation and its solution.

DEMAND INFLATION

Demand inflation occurs when — for whatever reason — the demand for goods and services in general exceeds the available supply. This

---

[1] Actually the separation of level and structure is not this easy. For example: (1) given existing economic institutions, some prices are necessarily fixed by contract; thus all prices cannot change together, so that inflation necessarily alters relative prices, redistributing both income and wealth, with further repercussions on the pressure of inflation; (2) under many circumstances, a force which operates initially to change relative prices may set off a general inflation (e.g., an excess demand for a particular kind of labor may generate wage increases which then spread to other kinds of labor and produce generalized upward price movement). However, for purposes of the present paper, which necessarily paints with a broad brush, such considerations are ignored.

[2] Prof. A. P. Lerner uses the terms "buyers' inflation" and "sellers' inflation" to distinguish them.

case involves the assumption that individual prices, including wage rates, tend to rise in direct and immediate response (and only in response) to an excess of market demand over supply. An excess demand for a few individual commodities or types of labor or in a few localities does not produce inflation. For there may be excess supply some place else and prices may be falling. So long as the excess demand is specific and localized, individual prices or wages may rise. Presumably, however, they will not often rise very fast or very far, and never without limit, because their rise will tend to cause buyers of the product or users of the service to shift to another directly or indirectly competitive product or service, the price of which has not risen, or may even be falling. And the increased rewards obtainable in the production or sale of the commodity in short supply will cause resources to be diverted into its production from production of other products. Both the diversion of patronage away from the product and the diversion of resources into it tend to eliminate the excess demand and limit the rise in price.

Only when there is a generalized excess demand does inflation threaten; for then there are not stable-priced substitutes to attract away the excess demands for individual products as their prices rise; and there are no idle resources to be attracted away from other uses, eliminating the deficiencies of supply.

Demand inflation arises when the demand for goods-in-general — that is, the demands for most particular goods and services — exceeds the supply of goods-in-general — that is, the supplies of most particular goods and services, "when all productive resources are fully employed."

This view of the nature of inflation is not confined to any one school of economists — for example, the "Keynesians." The older-fashioned quantity theory approach, which emphasizes the role of the quantity of money, equally visualizes inflation as proceeding from excess demand. The quantity theory view merely stresses a close connection between the quantity of money and the demand for goods in general. I prefer not to emphasize this connection — I believe that the relationship of money to total demand for goods is more tenuous, or, at best, slower in manifesting itself, than do some of my colleagues; I stress other connections as being more important, or at least more strategic. But these differences do not really matter for my argument here.

What I am concerned with here is not the reason for the excess demand, but rather that this kind of inflation proceeds from the free-market response of individual prices and wages to supply and demand considerations. In particular, it is assumed that most or all individual prices and wages are freely flexible, and respond by rising when and only when demand exceeds supply.

One may accept this view without its counterpart. The counterpart is, of course, that wages and prices respond directly and immediately by falling whenever supply exceeds demand. This would mean that generalized excess supply could never exist except in the presence of general and rapid deflation. Since this is so contrary to experience, we may often describe the behavior at least of wage rates as inflexible downward — i. e., stable when supply exceeds demand — but quick to rise in the reverse situation. A decline in the demand for goods-in-general need not always create an excess supply of goods; production may be cut back as fast as demand declines, creating only an excess supply of labor. Unemployment of labor, however, probably does not produce very rapid or appreciable decline of wage rates.

CONTROL OF DEMAND INFLATION

If we have demand inflation, the remedy is to reduce demand so that it no longer exceeds supply. This can be done by monetary policy, if and to the extent that the supply of money directly influences the demand for goods; or it can be done by fiscal policy; reduced Government purchasing reduces demand directly, and tax increases reduce it indirectly by reducing consumer or business after-tax incomes. It is not so easy as it sometimes sounds, because time is required to make any of these measures effective. This requires that we either guess as to the strength of future demand, or else make things as automatic and prompt as possible by arranging for the appropriate monetary or fiscal action to be tied automatically to some price index. But despite the difficulties, demand inflation can, at least conceptually, be simply handled — just reduce demand until the excess disappears.

This approach reserves for a minor qualification the circumstance that there are numerous "frictions" and "immobilities." These mean that the general price level may begin to rise sharply from excess demand while there still exists some margin of unemployment. An excess demand for many or most goods (and thus for the resources that produce them) can exist side by side with pockets of idle workers, or plants with excess capacity. This will be the case to the extent that moderately rising wages where there are labor scarcities fail immediately to pull unemployed workers away from the localities and occupations where there are surpluses of labor; and also to the extent that only a large rise in the prices of the scarce goods can divert enough demand toward the areas of excess supply to utilize fully their idle productive capacity. Thus, even in wartime unemployment never fell below about 600,000, despite intense inflationary pressure. We cannot aim at absolutely full employment, or even 98 percent employment, unless we are willing to accept considerable inflation. By increasing the mobility of labor (and other resources), perhaps we can raise the demand inflation point from, say, 96 percent of full employment to 98 percent; but 100 percent is impossible.

But we shall not dwell on the frictional problem here. We only recognize that it slightly complicates the demand inflation picture. Aside from this, the demand inflation analysis sees the price level rising whenever total demand exceeds the full-employment capacity of the economy, stable when demand is just sufficient for full employment, and either stable or falling if total demand is short of full employment output. It sees control of inflation as involving the limitation of demand through monetary and fiscal policy.

COST INFLATION

Cost inflation has almost invariably been described as stemming from labor-union pressure on wage rates. It is wage-cost inflation. This analysis recognizes that wage rates in the modern economy are not strictly market-determined prices. They do not adjust quickly and freely and automatically to whatever level may be necessary to "clear" the labor market. They are administered prices, and, as such, do not rise only when the demand for labor exceeds the supply. This recognition carries one step further the concession made to realism when we assume that, although wages and prices rise in response to excess demand, they do not fall whenever there exists any unemployment. I shall argue at a later point that this wage-cost inflation analysis is still lopsided, and thus misleading, by recognizing that wage rates are administered prices but failing to recognize that most prices for goods and services are also administered. (I use the term "administered prices" in a completely neutral sense: they are not necessarily bad or good, high or low, collusive or competitive; they are merely prices that are set by a seller, or buyer, and maintained unchanged for a considerable period, rather than being determined like prices of wheat or cotton or General Motors shares by continuous bid and offer.) But first we will review the usual analysis of wage-cost inflation.

We now recognize that rising wage rates are not exclusively the product of an excess demand for labor. We see that collective bargaining produces wage rates that rise even when there is no excess demand for labor — perhaps even an excess supply. Wage rates tied to the cost of living fall in this category, as do wages which automatically rise in reflection of some presumed (or even measured) rise in productivity. Wage rates which rise because employers can afford to pay them are in this group, or which rise because employers want their workers to be happy. Wage rates which rise to preserve parity with wages elsewhere or for other kinds of labor are also in this class, as well as wage rates that rise simply because organized workers are able by successful strike or threat of strike, to compel employers to pay the higher rates. The crucial difference from the previous case is that here rising wages are not, for each and every type of labor and in each and every labor market or even in the typical cases, confined to the situation in which there is an actual, experienced market scarcity of labor, which forces employers to compete for workers by bidding wages upward.

Suppose that employers generally should agree to or be forced to raise wage rates even when there was no scarcity of labor. If the rise exceeds the slow improvement or productivity, this raises employers' costs of production and, on normal assumptions, would reduce their willingness to supply goods at the previously prevailing price level. A reduction of supply would not be accompanied by an equivalent reduction of demand, and prices for products would thus rise. Unless and until prices rose in the same proportion as wage rates there would exist a tendency for the supply of goods to fall short of demand, thus causing the price rise to continue until the previous ratio of wages to prices was restored.[3]

In fact, we know that what is more likely to happen is that such wage increases will lead employers directly to post higher price tags,

[3] In the above paragraph I have summarized, without explanation, a fairly complex theoretical argument. Briefly set forth, the usual treatment assumes that (a) employers determine prices and outputs in a way which continually maximizes short-period profits; and (b) the "marginal revenue product" of labor declines for each firm as employment and output increase. These assumptions mean that if wage rates are raised, employers will not offer the previous volume of employment (producing the previous volume of output) unless or until prices rise in equal proportion, restoring the previous "real wage." The conclusion that demand for total output will fall by less than output, and thus assure the necessary rise in prices, assumes (a) that the "marginal propensity to consume" is (in "real" terms) less than unit, and (b) that any change in current wages and prices revises investors' expectations of future wages and prices in the same degree (i.e., the "elasticity of expectations" is unity). It, however, ignores (see fourth paragraph following) the possible effect on aggregate demand — presumably via interest rates — of a failure of the quantity of money to expand proportionately. As indicated, I think this is a matter of secondary importance.

rather than first to reduce their supply and let the market bid prices up. But even if prices of goods rise only in response to an actual excess of demand over supply, one can reach the conclusion (based on the assumptions summarized in the footnote to the preceding paragraph) that prices would be bid up in the proportion that wage rates rose.

This is spontaneous inflation. It requires no excess demand; it can even occur when there is some or perhaps considerable unemployment. It arises because wages increase even with no excess demand for labor.

Now there are two objections often made to this argument. One is that wages cannot and will not rise unless there is a genuine excess demand for labor — that the labor market really behaves like the purely competitive market of economic theory — that the demand inflation case is the only case. This view argues that labor gets wage increases only when there exists a true scarcity of labor. I do not believe that most employers would accept this observation and neither would most unions; nor can I agree that it is a correct description of wage determination. To be sure labor does get wage increases when there is a labor scarcity — larger increases than when there is no scarcity; but wage increases also occur for classes of labor for which there is no excess demand, and perhaps even when there are no classes of labor in excess demand.

The second objection is that any rise in the general level of wages and prices, unless it is accompanied by at least a proportional expansion of the money supply,[4] will reduce the total demand for goods. This reduction in demand will create unemployment, and the development of unemployment will quickly put an end to inflationary wage hikes. There is merit in this objection, but, in my judgment, not much. In the first place, I do not think that the reduction in demand accompanying a moderate inflation of the price level will be very great, even if the money supply does not expand.[5] Second, even if there is a reduction of demand which creates unemployment, the

---

[4] Or an increase in Government deficits.

[5] Some argue that the monetary authorities will necessarily have to "ratify" the inflation by increasing the money supply; or even that the "necessary" increase in money will come more or less automatically. Since I do not consider the change in money supply of much short-run importance (there was no change, for example, from 1955 to 1957). I prefer not to stress this aspect. Of course, there are limits to the increase in "velocity" that occurs if prices rise and output does not fall while money supply is constant. But they are likely to be reached or to have their effects at a point in time sufficiently remote from the wage increase as to be for all practical purposes an independent event.

level of unemployment sufficient to eliminate inflationary wage increases is probably fairly high. Thus, even if inflation should eventually curb itself, it would have to proceed rather far before the curb would work. We probably would find both the extent of the inflation and the degree of the necessary unemployment socially intolerable.

CONTROL OF WAGE COST INFLATION

It is commonly agreed that this kind of inflation is much more difficult to control by traditional monetary or fiscal means than demand inflation. For to avoid it, aggregate demand must be kept or pushed low enough, and sufficient unemployment created, that unions will not seek or else employers will refuse to grant — strike or no strike — wage increases in excess of productivity increases. This may mean a very considerable body of unemployment. Even if it does not, it may require a sacrifice of the rate of economic growth that we want. For, in this view, fiscal and monetary measures can control inflation only by putting pressure on the employer, in order that he may in turn put pressure on the union. Employers' profits are thus caught between the upper millstone of a restrictive monetary or fiscal policy, operating to reduce aggregate demand, and the lower millstone of upward wage pressure. Profits must be squeezed until employers are able and willing to squeeze the inflation out of wage demands. This may be disastrous for investment and thus for growth.

Recognition of these difficulties is why some businessmen appear to have decided that they would prefer a little inflation. Others have concluded that control of upward wage pressure must come not from fiscal or monetary policy, but from a direct attack on the strength of unions, through new labor legislation. Personally, I do not believe that proposed changes in labor laws (short of abolition of collective bargaining) would have much effect on upward wage pressures: right-to-work laws may only make unions more aggressive in seeking wage increases; prohibition of industry-wide bargaining may weaken employers as much or more than unions; and so on. However, I shall not pursue this point.

THE TWO TYPES OF INFLATION CANNOT BE DISTINGUISHED IN PRACTICE

Economists have talked so much about these two kinds of inflation in recent years that it seems to me strange that they have not been able to say more about what has been happening. In particular, I would like to know to what extent the inflation in the United States since the war has been demand inflation and to what extent, if any, it has been wage-cost inflation. I find very little discussion and no agreement on this question. Take it year by year. We can probably agree to throw the price increases between 1945 and 1947 and between 1950 and 1951 into the demand-inflation category, although I assert that it is very hard to prove this to be the case. These 3 years account for about five-eighths of the total inflation of 56 percent in the cost of living over the period 1945–57. What about the other years of smaller price increase: 1948, 1952, 1953, 1956, and 1957? Why is there debate about these years? Why is it hard to prove that even in 1946, 1947, and 1951 the rise in prices was demand-induced?

Let us see how we should expect wages and prices to behave in a year of demand inflation and how this behavior would differ in a year of cost inflation. In the demand inflation case, presumably it is an excess demand in the product markets that pulls or bids prices upward. The increased profitability of production in turn creates an excess demand in the labor market which bids or pulls wage rates upward. The fact that wages are set by collective bargaining rather than in a hypothetical free competitive market does not, of course, mean that wages cannot rise through an excess demand for labor.[6] In any case, in demand inflation, excess product demand pulls up goods prices, creating excess labor demand which pulls up wages.

In the wage-cost inflation case it is turned around. Wage rates rise without excess demand, which creates an actual or potential shortage of supply of goods (at the old price level). This shortage bids up prices (or would bid them up if sellers didn't automatically advance them).

The reason why it is difficult to distinguish the two cases in practice is that neither prices nor wages are set in a way that permits us to make the theoretical distinctions we require. Given the way wages are actually determined we find it difficult to answer the question: Would this much of a rise in wages have occurred even if wages had been set by an auction method? Nor, given the way most prices are actually set, can we answer the question: Would prices have risen as they did — i. e., would they have been bid up by excess demand — even if wages had not risen?

The fact is that most prices are not set by impersonal supply and demand forces any more than wage rates are. For some farm prod-

[6] It may be, however, as some have suggested, that in highly demand-inflationary situations the institution of collective bargaining actually slows up the increase in wage rates.

ucts and raw materials, prices do respond directly and almost daily to demand and supply considerations. Prices rise when demand exceeds supply, and only when it does, and fall in the reverse case. But for most manufactured goods and for almost all goods and services at the retail level, prices rise and fall not in direct reflection of impersonal supply and demand forces, but instead in response to some person's decision, applying some rule or formula or using his informed judgment as to the best way to behave in the current situation.

The general price level rose in 1956 and 1957. This general rise consisted of increases in millions of individual prices, which more than offset reductions in a few prices and stability in many others. Was the rise in most of these prices in response to an excess of demand over supply? How do we know? How could we ever find out? The very concept — clear enough in the economics textbooks — is almost impossible to apply in most markets.

Among others, prices of steel and of automobiles rose. Were these particular increases the result of excess demand? That is, had the price of steel not been revised upward by a deliberate policy decision, would the market have bid prices up? And would it have been by the particular number of dollars a ton that actually occurred? To ask the question in this form is to show that it is not fully answerable. We can perhaps look for some indicators of the presence of excess demand in each of the postwar years — as revealed, for example, in order backlogs. However, we would need to know not only whether there were order backlogs (there are probably always some), but how general they were, how extensive, and for how long they were expected to last. With this information, and knowledge of the extent to which productive capacity was currently employed, we might be able to determine that some of the price increases that have occurred in steel since the war were probably in response to excess demand; others clearly occurred with no excess of demand over supply; regarding still other instances, it would be impossible to reach a judgment. In hardly any case could we guess whether the particular price increase that did occur was of a magnitude approximating what would have occurred in a market in which price adjusted automatically to supply and demand.

In some ways the steel case is a relatively easy one, for the concept of "capacity" may have fairly definite meaning in steel. But consider automobiles. Not only does the output of each make of automobile often move independently of other makes, but what does "capacity" mean for any single make? With how many assembly lines operating, at what speed, for how many shifts, and for how many months (prospectively) of the year?[7] The concepts required by the contrast of demand and wage cost inflation are no easier to apply to most other manufactured products — appliances, clothing, processed foods, chemicals, rubber products, and so forth.

We simply find it extremely difficult to say that, in 1957, prices would have gone up even if wages hadn't, and this pulled wages up; or, on the contrary, prices would not have gone up if wages hadn't — the wage inflation forced prices up. It is not only that we cannot say that one or the other was true of most markets; it is even very hard to say which was the case in any single market.

But it is worse than this. It is not merely that we cannot tell what is the case in a particular time and place. The distinction itself tends to break down when we bring the real-world processes of price and wage setting into our consideration. What does it mean any longer to say that in 1951 we had demand inflation because wages rose no more than they would have been bid up in an auction-type labor market (given the rises in goods prices that were occurring), when the rises in goods prices that were occurring were predicated in most instances, through markup formulas or the exercise of "good business judgment," on the simultaneous and expected rise in wage rates? Or what does it mean to say that in 1957 we had cost inflation because prices rose no more than they would have been expected to rise in response to demand-supply forces, given the rise in wage costs that occurred in 1957, when this very rise in wage costs was at least in part tied (through cost-of-living clauses or the cost-of-living principle in wage negotiation) to the rise in prices that was occurring or was expected to occur in 1957?

In short, the dichotomy between demand and cost inflation appears to break down in application. The principal reason why it breaks down is that neither in the labor market nor in most commodity markets are wages or prices set in automatic response to supply-demand forces, rising when and only when there is an immediate current excess of demand over supply. Perhaps this breakdown should not surprise us. It would not surprise the housewife. On the contrary,

[7] It is well known that the concept of a "supply curve" has no meaning under oligopoly conditions. However, even if we measure "supply" by a curve of average or marginal costs, we could give clear meaning to an assessment of the presence of excess demand only if the cost curve were rectangular, or nearly so: flat up to some limit of output where it rises vertically, or at least with a sharp discontinuity. I do not know how to conceptualize the supply curve for automobiles. But even the marginal cost curve (of each make) is surely not rectangular, and we cannot merely compare demand with "capacity."

she would be astonished to be told that two distinctly different kinds of inflation had been alternately operating on her budget during the postwar period. The only difference she observes is that in some years prices have risen faster than in others. Would it not be more reasonable for us to look for an analysis of inflation which does not require the assumption that two different kinds of things have been happening to prices in the postwar period?

In such an analysis aggregate demand must play an important role. I certainly do not wish to argue that aggregate demand has no relevance to inflation; this would be absurd. I merely say that the concept is not useful — not operational — in the form in which it is usually presented. We can perhaps meaningfully compare two states of aggregate demand. Within limits, we can decide that demand was probably greater in one year than another. But can we meaningfully — that is, operationally — compare demand with supply? As will be seen below, my treatment, in effect, makes demand inflation a matter of degree, not of kind.

The usual wage-cost inflation analysis has the advantage that it recognizes, realistically, that wages are administered prices; but, unrealistically, it assumes at least tacitly either that prices of goods and services are market-determined rather than administered, or that this makes no difference. I believe it necessary to recognize explicitly that prices as well as wages are "administered." My second criticism of the usual wage-cost inflation analysis is that it ignores the fact that not only do prices follow wages but that wages also follow prices. Today's wage increase may seem to require tomorrow's price increase. But, to labor, today's wage increase was an important measure required by yesterday's increase in the cost of living. We are talking about the behavior of wages and prices during periods of inflation. This means a rising cost of living. We certainly cannot forget rising prices in discussing rising wage rates.

Is there any alternative theoretical analysis which provides a better insight into the nature of the inflationary process and the policies necessary to control it? There is a third such analysis, usually — and I think mistakenly — condemned by economists as unsound.

MARKUP INFLATION

I shall present a very simplified version of what I call the "markup" analysis of inflation, indicate the criticisms made of this approach and why I think that they are mistaken, then elaborate the analysis slightly. Finally, I shall consider its implications for economic policy.

Suppose that all business firms have the practice of pricing the goods and services which they sell on the basis of some standard markup over their costs of materials and labor. For the moment, assume constant efficiency or productivity. Suppose, further, that labor seeks and is able to get wage increases to match any increase in the level of consumer prices. In effect labor, too, then prices its services on the basis of a fixed markup over its cost of living.

Now it is easy to see that this model can generate either a stable, a rising, or a falling price level, depending on the markups which business and labor respectively employ. The markup pattern by business may be such that a wage level of $2 an hour yields a price index of 100, which was just the index level which led workers to demand a wage level of $2. But this need not be the case. Suppose that a wage level of $2 leads to a price index of 104, and that a price index of 104 leads workers to seek and to get a wage of $2.08, which in turn requires a price index of 108.2, a wage level of $2.164, and so on. Clearly an endless upward spiral of wages and prices would ensue so long as these bases for setting wages and prices prevailed. If the markup on one or both sides is a percentage markup, the inflation will proceed faster than if one or both of the markups is fixed in dollars and cents. Further, depending on the magnitudes of the two markups, the spiral may eventually taper off into stability (in the absence of a new push) or may have no termination. These are matters of detail, dear to the heart of a mathematical model builder, but of no great relevance here. The important fact is that, if each participant prices on the basis of a markup over the prices he pays, we can have a spiraling process of very considerable magnitude and duration.

This spiral works within the business sector as well as between business as a whole and labor. Most sales by the "average" business firm are made to another business firm. If one firm raises its prices in order to preserve its desired markup, this raises the costs of other firms, which in turn raise their prices, increasing the costs of still other firms (including perhaps the initial firm), in an endless chain. Some of the sales of some of these firms are also made to consumers. This raises the cost of living and, by causing wage costs also to rise, intensifies the spiral. Nevertheless, it should be noted that the dollar value of sales between business firms is much greater than the dollar value of sales of labor to firms. Even if wage rates were stable, we could have a considerable round of markup inflation entirely within the business sector, if the markups applied by firms were such as to produce it.

Now it is also clear that even if the markups applied by business and by labor were such as to produce an inflationary spiral, a gradual improvement of efficiency and productivity might eventually bring the spiral to a halt. For a rise in efficiency means that a rise in wage rates or prices of purchased materials produces a smaller rise in labor and materials costs. Thus markup patterns which were initially inconsistent with stable prices can become consistent with stability through the growth of productivity.

But this happy result would, of course, be lost, if the several parties to the game each tried to appropriate the gains of rising productivity, through expansion of their markups. Indeed, if the desired shares of the productivity gain add up to 100 percent — or, as they easily might, to more than 100 percent — of the gains of productivity increase, the spiral might still go on indefinitely. And this effort to expand the markups to appropriate some of the gains of rising productivity is just what we observe. Labor seeks not merely to maintain a constant "real wage," but to achieve a rising standard of living; business, too, would like to enjoy some of the benefits of the increasing productivity which, one must agree, arise primarily from business investment and managerial skill and ingenuity. (One time-honored way in which this occurs is through the application of customary markups to "standard" costs, using current wages rates and materials prices. Unless the "standards" are revised to reflect the rising productivity, this appropriates the entire productivity gain to management.)

Now our model is dreadfully oversimplified. But we can expand it without changing greatly the conclusions. For example, we can add an agricultural sector. However, if we have agricultural prices supported at some percentage of parity, this only adds to the inflationary race, particularly because our parity index assumes that farmers should receive 100 per cent of the gains that occur in agricultural productivity. There should also be added a free-market sector, in which prices respond freely to supply-and-demand forces, a sector largely identified with raw materials. Imports and exports get into the picture, too. These greatly complicate the analysis and succeed primarily in obscuring rather than altering the primary engine of inflation. This engine is the struggle between labor and business to preserve levels of return and to achieve gains in return that cannot be accommodated out of the total national income. It is as if the two parties were demanding shares of the national income that added up to more than 100 percent of the total national income. The attempt of each to get his desired "fair share" produces only an indefinite inflationary spiral.

There is no evidence that either labor or business wants inflation as such; indeed each deplores it. The goal of business in setting prices is not to get higher prices; it is to obtain what it considers a "fair" markup over costs; if costs went down, so would prices. When businessmen raise prices, they often do it apologetically, explaining that they are no more than reflecting the rise that has occurred in their costs — or even showing that their price increase falls short of the increase in their costs (as did both President Curtice, of General Motors, and Vice President Yntema, of Ford, in recent testimony). The implication is clear that the passing along to buyers of cost increases (or decreases), i. e., the preservation of a markup, is taken as the normal and obvious standard by which the propriety of a price change should be judged.

Nor does labor seek inflation. What it wants is a standard of living protected against erosion from higher prices, and increasing gradually to reflect labor's "fair share" of the gains of rising productivity.

One thing that appeals to me about the markup hypothesis is that it places the emphasis where unions and businessmen place it, not on the level of prices, per se, nor on supply and demand, but on the preservation of "fair" relationships between buying prices (including the cost-of-living), and selling prices (including wage rates).

OBJECTIONS TO THE MARKUP ANALYSIS

The hypothesis that most prices are set by markup over cost is often rejected as meaningless by economists. This may be the superficial form that pricing takes, they agree; nevertheless, the markups used are not just any numbers that come into the sellers' minds. The markups employed merely reflect the operation of more fundamental supply and demand forces, and change as these forces change. If sellers in a given field try to use markups that are too high, they will find themselves unable to sell what they expected to be able to sell at the prices they are charging; inventories will pile up; prices (and thus markups) will be adjusted downward.

If the analysis is of prices in their aspect of structure — in connection with problems of resource allocation and income distribution — this objection has real merit, and the markup hypothesis may not be useful, even as a starting point. But the objection is not equally relevant to an analysis of the inflationary process. If sellers typically set prices by applying customary markups to their costs, then in an inflationary setting of generally rising costs, relative prices and markups need not change appreciably as the price level rises. And even if they do change, some markups are as likely to be revised upward as others are downward. As a description of the way in which price levels change, the markup hypothesis is neither meaningless nor far from the truth; it is certainly a more realistic and useful hypothesis than the assumption that prices adjust immediately and directly to a "clear-the-market" level set by supply and demand.

Nevertheless, the fact is that markups do vary, and their variation is significant. If our interest is in price structure we are concerned (in effect) with variations in relative markups — how markups fall in those fields in which supply tends to exceed demand and rise where demand tends to exceed supply. But this concentration on relative markups has led us to neglect consideration of the general average or level of markups. It is my hypothesis that this is precisely where total demand becomes relevant to an analysis of the price level. I suggest that it is a useful hypothesis that the average level of markups employed by business firms rises as total demand increases and falls as demand declines.[8]

The second related hypothesis I make is that the "markup" which unions (and employers) apply to the cost-of-living in setting wage rates also tends to rise and fall as the volume of unemployment falls and rises.

This modification of the markup analysis of inflation makes it, I think, a more fruitful tool. It shows why inflation may occur, even with some slack in the economy; but it also indicates why inflationary difficulties becomes more intense as total demand increases. It provides, I think, a framework which embraces elements both of the demand and of the cost analyses.

Too much of our thinking about inflation has concentrated on how it starts rather than with how it proceeds. Inflation might start from an initial "autonomous" increase either in business or labor

[8] A reader of a draft of this paper commented that this is just another way of saying that prices rise in response to excess demand. I do not think so. The question is not whether prices rise but when and by how much they rise and how this amount is determined. If prices are completely market-determined, varying daily or hourly to clear the market, then I agree that the excess demand theory answers our questions. But if this is not the case, we can talk meaningfully about the extent and pace and mechanics of inflation only by taking account of the particular ways in which prices are set. To say that prices rise "in response to" excess demand doesn't help much unless we know how far or how fast or how often they rise. My thesis is that the best simple and general description is to say that they rise when costs rise, usually not before; that the price rise tends to be about equal to the rise in costs at "moderate" levels of demand, somewhat greater (but not "much greater") when demand is at a higher level, somewhat (but not much) less when demand is lower.

markups. Or it might start from an increase in aggregate demand which first and most directly affected some of the flexible, market-determined prices. But, however it starts, the process involves both demand and markup elements.[9]

A fuller elaboration of our simple model should take account of additional elements, including particularly the role of expectations, both as to demand and as to cost, and by consumers as well as businessmen. However, I would insist that one principal relevance of expectations — except perhaps in hyper-inflations — is with respect to the cost base to which business markups are applied, or the rising cost of living assumed in wage negotiations. When demand is moderate, markups may be applied to historical, experienced costs. As demand increases and the pace of price rise accelerates, there is an increasing tendency to project rising labor and material prices into the future and to apply markups to these. Workers assume that the cost of living will rise, and try to anticipate it in their wage settlements. This is one reason, perhaps the principal one, why markups (over actual cost) rise with increases in aggregate demand.[10]

The other principal relevance of expectations is with respect to

[9] Dr. Franz B. Wolf, who kindly read a draft of this paper, makes the following comment, which I find so lucid that I cannot refrain from quoting it in full: "It probably can be shown that the apparent justification of classifying some periods of inflation one way and some the other is due not so much to differences in the process of inflation but to differences in the reaction of public policy. Under war conditions, fiscal, credit, and monetary policy is ineffective but markup control is enforced in greater degree against both business and labor; consequently, markup inflation is slowed down sharply and demand inflation proceeds under the surface and we speak of the period as one of demand inflation. In recent years, credit and monetary policy (and, to a lesser extent, fiscal policy) has curbed the demand inflation process but has been ineffective in curbing markup inflation; so we speak of the latter. In reality, under both conditions the entire process has continued, as the aspect which has remained unaffected by public policy has impaired the effect of public policy even on that aspect toward which it was directed.

"This may make it a little more difficult to distinguish between price control (which, inter alia, curbs increases in markups) and the remedy to be developed for the peacetime inflation process with its emphasis on markup inflation. But it should still be possible to make the distinction clear and to show that under all conditions (1) monetary and credit and fiscal policy can only combat that aspect which is now described as demand inflation, (2) demand inflation and markup inflation are in reality merely two aspects of an integrated process, and (3) the one aspect which is allowed to proceed will make the control of the other ineffective.

[10] An additional reason why markups expand with aggregate demand is that the extent of discounts from and "shading" of quoted prices decreases with improving business conditions. At retail, this takes the form of fewer special

the impact of price expectations on inventory behavior, both of consumers and firms, and upon the timing of investment decisions. Expectations have, of course, great importance for the movement of the relatively few demand-determined prices — the raw-materials prices which can (and often have) doubled or trebled in a few weeks of frantic trading.

Price expectations depend partly on recent price movements; but they can also be generated by news (of war, shortages, tax changes, etc.).

In summary, the advantage that I see in the markup analysis of inflation is that it focuses attention where attention belongs — on the wage policies of trade unions and the pricing policies of business firms, both of which can best be understood in terms of reaction to cost changes. The concept of prices that are set by impersonal supply and demand forces, to clear the market, rising in sensitive response to an excess of demand, and only under such conditions, is both operationally almost meaningless and completely unrealistic. It is just as useless and unrealistic as the assumption that wage rates are so determined. The existence of many "layers" of sales and resales within the business sector also seems to me to make it useful to focus attention on costs, and the pyramiding of costs.

CONTROL OF MARKUP INFLATION

In the light of the markup analysis, the tools of monetary and fiscal policy obviously can have some effect on inflation. A reduction of total demand for goods will tend to reduce the general level of markups which sellers apply to their costs; as a reduced total demand for goods is translated into reduced employment, the wage demands of trade unions tend to be scaled somewhat downward — or, if not the demands, the wage increases for which they are willing ultimately to settle.

But it is also clear that there is no neat relationship between full employment and inflation. Inflation may be a troublesome problem even (as in 1956 and 1957) with no general pressure on the labor

"sales" at "markdown" prices. I am convinced that the initial markups applied by sellers in computing their announced prices vary little between conditions of moderate prosperity and boom. The principal difference in realized markups occurs through the greater tendency for projection of cost increases during boom periods and through the greater prevalence of "sales" and special deals when demand slackens.

supply; inflation may even survive in weakened form (as perhaps in 1958) in a period when there is considerable slack in the economy.

In view of this unhappy state of affairs, is there nothing that can be done to avoid a gradual upward creep of the price level — a creep that becomes uncomfortably rapid whenever the economy is sustaining vigorous growth and full utilization of its potential, and which stops only when the economy performs badly in these other respects?

To answer this question, we need to remind ourselves why it is that the process of wage and price determination seems to be inconsistent with price stability, at least at full employment. The mere fact that both business and labor set their prices on the basis of a markup over costs, with an effort to capture some part of the gains of rising productivity, does not inevitably mean inflation. It means inflation only if the markups are inconsistent — if one or both of the markups is too high.

WHOSE MARKUP IS TOO HIGH?

The usual cost inflation analysis necessarily places the blame solely and squarely on labor. Inflation occurs when labor makes inflationary wage claims. The markup analysis qualifies this conclusion, by pointing out that it is the combination, the interaction, of wage claims and business pricing policies that may produce inflation.

It is not hard to see why labor is usually given the sole blame for inflation. First, in the usual cost inflation analysis, prices (but not wages) are assumed to be set by impersonal supply and demand forces. This leaves no one to blame (except labor) if prices rise. We see wages set in a conflict situation — by bargaining between workers (the inflationists) and employers (who are fighting for price stability). Prices, on the other hand, are traditionally set by unilateral determination. Both buyers and sellers formally participate in setting wage rates; only sellers in setting most other prices. We tend to see conflict only in a formal context of conflict. Second, most analyses of wage cost inflation gloss over the relation of the cost of living to wage demands. This is like asserting that the chicken necessarily comes before the egg. Thus, Vice President Yntema of Ford, in his recent testimony before the Senate Monopoly Subcommittee, talked about the wage increases in 1956 and 1957 which raised the costs of Ford cars, and forced price increases. But had Ford prices not increased (and prices charged by most other manufacturers similarly situated) wage rates would have increased very much less, because the cost-of-living escalator would not have operated.

Although labor gets most of the blame for inflation, labor stubbornly refuses to take the villain's role. Its wage demands are reasonable, Walter Reuther insists, and consistent with price stability, if only the cost of living were controlled, and if business did not insist on exorbitant profit demands.

The markup analysis of inflation requires us at least to face labor's question. We can no longer hide behind "supply and demand" as the determinant of all prices except the price of labor. We have inflation if the markups are inconsistent, but is only labor's markup too high?

I do not know the answer. I do not even know how one should judge whether business markups are too high. We would have a standard for this judgment if all industries were organized like the pure and perfect competition of our economics textbook. But they are not so organized, and I doubt that we would be satisfied if they were. For the markups which purely competitive sellers are able to apply to their costs would provide profit margins probably quite insufficient for the massive reinvestment of earnings which is so important to our economic growth, and the vast expenditures on research and development which are crucial to our economic progress.

But merely because we have no easy standard to judge their propriety, and merely because business margins serve an economic function related to growth and progress (as well as provide the income of the owning and managerial classes), we need not assume that whatever business markups may happen to be are necessarily correct and above examination. It seems to me that, a priori, it may be as sound to claim that business markups may be "too high" as to claim that wage demands may be excessive, as sound to blame business as labor for inflation.

What needs to be recognized is that it is the attempted or desired markups by labor and business which are "too high," individually or in combination. The actually realized markups can never be inconsistent. The two interest groups can lay claims that add up to more than 100 per cent of the national income; but they can never receive more than 100 per cent. It is inflation which chisels away the excess. To say that social policy should find a better way of chopping these inconsistent claims down to size is not to say that either group must necessarily take a smaller share of the national income than it is in fact getting.

WHAT WE CAN DO

The problem of inflation may very well be our No. 1 domestic economic problem in the years ahead. Thus I believe that the Joint Economic Committee can perform a great public service, through its present study, and otherwise, in contributing to the public understanding of the nature and seriousness of the problem. But mere understanding will not be enough. I have a feeling that some business and labor leaders realize, even better than many economists seem to do, what the real problem is. But they feel — and are — quite powerless to do anything about it. Even if all of the participants in the processes of wages and price setting fully understood the problem, it is not clear that there would be much that any of them, in their private capacities, could do. Public action seems to me to be required.

I do not have, nor do I think anyone has, sufficient knowledge or imagination to suggest what final form this action should take. Certainly wage and price controls of the wartime variety would be completely out of place. Yet at the other extreme mere talk is not enough, either.

It is clear that the public has a stake in the wage-setting and price-setting decisions that are responsible for inflation. All of us (and some groups in particular) are innocent bystanders who are getting hurt by the contestants in a game of musical chairs that no one does or can permanently win.

The public stake in these wage and price decisions does not get expressed unless someone expresses it. But vague exhortations, appealing for "restraint" in wage and price determination, such as have been frequently made by Presidents Truman and Eisenhower (most recently in the 1958 Economic Report), and by leading officials of their administrations, seem to me almost worse than useless. Do we not need some machinery by which the public stake in these private decisions can be more sharply defined and brought to bear in specific terms upon the concrete issues which arise?

Perhaps one approach might be for the Congress to establish a permanent Wage and Price Commission, charged with the responsibility of (a) formulating general standards for noninflationary wage and price decisions; (b) collecting the information necessary to apply these standards to particular strategic proposed increases of wages and prices; and (c) making public its findings. I would supply the Commission with the power of subpena, an adequate economic staff, and the authority, even, to require temporary postponement of specific wage and price increases pending the Commission's study. I do not see the Commission as having any authority to establish legal maximum wages or prices, but merely that of expressing in as concrete terms as possible its dispassionate and documented judgments as to what the general objective of price stability might seem to require in the settlement of specific issues.

The idea is not new; it has been proposed many times in the past. Walter Reuther recently proposed a price commission — which would have investigatory powers concerning strategic price increases. This is as one sided as the view which fastens all blame for inflation on organized labor. Mr. Reuther might be somewhat less enthusiastic about a commission which could furnish the public with an impartial analysis of the inflationary results of the kind of wage increases which his own union has in the past demanded, and today — even in the face of large unemployment among his members — continues to demand.

I do not mean to single out Mr. Reuther as the inflationary villain any more than I accept his designation of the General Motors Corp. for that role. I only say that the public stake in price stability requires that we go beyond name calling, finger pointing, and vague appeals.

STANDARDS FOR WAGES AND PRICES

The great task for the Wage and Price Commission would be to work toward the formulation of appropriate standards for the public appraisal of wage claims and markup practices. I do not think that any of us should have any illusion that this would be easy, or that the questions raised do not go to the very heart of the economic process. Wartime price and wage control standards would be almost totally irrelevant.

Prof. A. P. Lerner has proposed an agency empowered to set compulsory ceilings, at least on strategic wages and prices. Although I reject this approach, my Commission would have to consider seriously his proposed wage and price standards. With respect to wages he would allow rates to advance by an amount equal to the assumed productivity increment — 2 or 3 per cent per year. But wage rates of individual groups of workers could advance by more than this where the unemployment percentage of that group was half of the average percentage for the economy as a whole, while no increase at all would be permitted for groups whose unemployment percentage was twice the national average. With respect to prices, increases would be permitted for industries operating at capacity, regardless of the level of profits; price decreases would be required for industries operating considerably below capacity (again, regardless of profits or losses). For cases between these limits, prices could not be raised.

Enforcement of these proposed standards would require incredibly complex determinations of the appropriate units (on the labor side, is the unit an industry, a firm, an area, a type of skill? on the price side, is the unit a firm, a product, an industry, or a regional segment?). Price and wage control experience in particular suggests the impossibility of either the product or the industry concept as a regulatory framework. But I have more fundamental objections. First, the concept of "capacity" is not an operational one, at least in most industries. I do not believe that it can be given even rough measurement. Second, the standard ignores materials costs which in some industries comprise 50, 60, or even 90 per cent of the price. These may rise for many reasons (increases in suppliers' prices permitted under the capacity rule, raw materials increases — clearly not subject to Lerner's control scheme, import prices, and so forth). Prices must at some point be allowed to rise to reflect materials cost, even if the industry is not at capacity. Similarly, an industry in which productivity increases by less than the national average would experience rising labor costs, which could not be ignored. Finally, I believe that Lerner dodges the fundamental question, which is the determination of appropriate "shares" for labor and capital. For example, in a prosperous, full-employment economy, many industries would be operating at or near capacity. Why should we assume that the proposed rule would produce as many price rollbacks as increases? If prices generally rose (and profits, too), could or should we ask labor to absorb increases in the cost of living?

I believe that Professor Lerner's suggested standards might serve as a starting point for the proposed Commission's work. But they are not the final answer. An attempt at their use in establishing compulsory ceilings would be beyond the competence of any administrative staff. This is one (but not the only) reason why I prefer the less drastic approach of an agency with only investigatory powers. I would foresee the Commission proceeding from the relatively obvious cases toward the more difficult, closer cases, evolving and refining its standards and procedures in the process. But it would avoid as the plague any effort to become an agency of mediation or compromise.

The difficulties in the way of a solution to the problem of inflation are clearly enormous. But if we mean business about price stability and full employment, it seems to me that it is high time to begin to explore our way, in some new directions, toward a solution.

PART THREE

ARE WAGE GUIDEPOSTS THE ANSWER?

FRITZ MACHLUP

Another View of Cost-Push and Demand-Pull Inflation*

Unlike Ackley, who contends that wages and prices chase each other upwards without the restrictive force of growing unemployment, Machlup holds that cost-push inflation faces the limiting barriers of declining sales and rising unemployment. This fundamental difference between the two views stems from their approach to the question of the determination of the levels of production and employment. While Ackley's analysis implies a macroeconomic examination, implicit in Machlup's analysis are microeconomic considerations.

Nowhere is Machlup's microeconomic approach more evident than in his treatment of the varying effects of increased productivity on prices and employment. When productivity increases in a single industry by 10 per cent, if the industry lowers its product prices by 10 per cent, then over a given period of time, the extra 10 per cent of output produced will be purchased by the rest of the economy, which, under Machlup's implied assumption of unitary elasticity of

* Reprinted by permission of the publishers from *The Review of Economics and Statistics*, Vol. XLII, No. 2 (May 1960), pp. 125–139, Cambridge, Mass.: Harvard University Press. Copyright 1960 by the President and Fellows of Harvard College.

demand for the product, will spend the same dollar amount as before. The gains in productivity of a particular industry are enjoyed in the form of increased real income to all because of the lowered prices of the industry experiencing the productivity gain. In this industry, employment is maintained at the previous levels, and factors associated with it are able to buy their own production more cheaply than before.

On the other hand, if the productivity gain in the industry is accompanied by an equivalent rise in factor payments, with no reduction in prices, then demand for the product will be the same as before; production and factor costs (incomes) remain unchanged, but there now arises a 10 per cent rise in unemployment among factors associated with the industry. The gains from productivity have been appropriated by the factors lucky enough to stay employed, at the cost of the unemployed factors. To reemploy these idled factors requires inflationary fiscal or monetary steps; hence Machlup's conclusion that a full-employment policy under conditions of increasing productivity, with the productivity gain taking the form of higher factor returns rather than lowered prices, leads to inflation.

Consider a macroeconomic approach to the effects of increasing productivity. If productivity gains are accompanied by lowered prices, then the volume of sales will increase. Sales will rise as prices fall, not because of the workings of classical wage theories, under which the economy can be stimulated by falling factor returns and prices, but because with rising productivity as prices fall factor returns do not fall. If the productivity gains are accompanied by constant prices with higher factor returns, then sales volume will again increase. Sales rise at constant prices, not because of any fortunate coincidental rise in aggregate demand, but because with increasing productivity at constant prices factor incomes have risen. With a positive marginal propensity to save, not all the increased income will result in increased consumption demand. Also, under the declining price framework, not all the increased real income thus created may be consumed.

The effects on demand are similar in the aggregate whether real income rises because of a fall in prices, factor income remaining unchanged, or because of increased factor income, prices remaining unchanged. Considering productivity increases industry by industry, as Machlup does, it is true that when an industry lowers its prices its sales will increase, and when productivity rises it can afford to lower its prices. The industry will not try to sell more at the old price—the alternative to reducing price in order to maintain full employment without recourse to outside inflationary steps—because it does not see any reason to believe that it can increase its sales volume. But considering the economy as a whole, productivity gains raise real income and production under conditions of unchanging spending propensities. While it is deflationary for this real income gain to take the form of lowered prices, it is not inflationary if a pattern of constant prices and higher money incomes results.

Acceptance of Machlup's position leads to two radical conclusions. In the first place, a policy of linking wage increases to productivity gains would have to be considered inherently inflationary. The policy does not in itself tend to raise prices, but matching changes in factor returns, industry by industry, distorts the national wage structure while matching by the national productivity movement is detrimental to the price-profit structure.

Secondly, and more seriously, an increase in productivity would have to be viewed pessimistically, as a force which increases unemployment. Sudden sharp productivity gains in particular industries can lead to technological unemployment. But technological unemployment is usually defined as a form of unemployment resulting from changes in productive techniques. Under true technological unemployment, the number of job applicants relative to the number of unfilled positions remains unchanged. A shift in productive technique has much the same effect on employment as a shift in demand from one sector to another. In Machlup's terminology, however, technological unemployment is equated with cyclical unemployment, and in his analysis this type of unemployment, and consequent inflationary steps to remedy it, would arise unless productivity gains were accompanied by lower prices. Acknowledgment of the fact that prices are reluctant to move downwards leads to the dreary conclusion that gains in productivity bring economic difficulties rather than provide the means of increasing output and raising living standards. The contributions made by productivity gains to economic growth in the United States stand as strong evidence against this conclusion.

Iᴛ is with some hesitation that I join the discussion and thus contribute to the galloping inflation of the literature on the creeping inflation of prices. My excuse is probably the same as that of most of my fellow writers: dissatisfied with much of what others have written, I have, perhaps presumptuously, decided that my way of thinking would be more successful. Hence, I am presenting another view of cost-push and demand-pull inflation.

THE CURRENT DEBATE

Before I set forth the controversial issue and the most widely held views, I shall indulge in a few preliminaries by referring briefly to the old squabble about what should be meant by inflation.

Inflation of What?

Some people regard "inflation" as a *cause* (explanation) of a general rise in prices (and of some other things too), while others use the word as a *synonym* (equivalent) for a general rise in prices. In times when governments undertake to control prices by prohibitions with threats of sanctions against unauthorized price raising, many writers realize how awkward it is to use the term inflation to signify price increase, because then they want to discuss the "latent" or "repressed" inflation — one that does not show up in a general price index, or does not show up adequately. Also when one talks about inflation and deflation as apparent opposites, a definition in terms of general prices is quite inconvenient, inasmuch as the problem of deflation is so serious largely because it shows up in falling volumes of production and employment instead of falling prices.

One solution would be to use the word inflation always with a modifying word that tells exactly what is blown up: currency, credit, spending, demand, wages, prices, etc. This would be a great help; indeed some controversial problems would disappear, because the disputants would find out that they were talking about different things, and other problems would be greatly clarified. The most lively issue of our times, whether "our" inflation in the last four years has been due to a demand pull or to a cost push, would lose some of its muddiness if the analysts had to qualify all their pronouncements with regard to the inflation of credit, spending, demand, wholesale prices, consumer prices, and so forth.

A search of the learned literature would yield scores of definitions of inflation, differing from one another in essentials or in nuances. A search of the popular literature, however, reveals no realization of the differences in the meanings experts give to the term. The differences apparently have been reserved for the treatises and the quarterlies; the daily papers and the weeklies were not to be encumbered with "technicalities." Now that inflation has become such a widely debated topic, with many scholars participating in the debates, the popular meaning of inflation, denoting an increase in the consumer price index, has been increasingly adopted by the professional economists. Although this is probably bad for analysis, we may have to accept it. But at the risk of appearing pedantic I shall continue to speak of various kinds of inflation and to specify which I happen to be speaking about.

The Controversial Issue

Opinion is divided on whether consumer prices in recent years have increased chiefly (1) because industry has invested too much and government has spent too much (relative to the nation's thrift) or (2) because big business has raised material prices and/or big labor has raised wage rates too high (relative to the nation's increase in productivity). The issue is partly who is to be "blamed" for the past rise in consumer prices, and partly what policies should be pursued to avoid a continued increase.

If demand-pull inflation is the correct diagnosis, the Treasury is to be blamed for spending too much and taxing too little, and the Federal Reserve Banks are to be blamed for keeping interest rates too low and for creating or tolerating too large a volume of free reserves, which enable member banks to extend too much credit.

If cost-push inflation is the correct diagnosis, trade unions are to be blamed for demanding excessive wage increases, and industry is to be blamed for granting them, big business may be blamed for raising "administered prices" of materials and other producers goods to yield ever-increasing profit rates, and government may be assigned the task of persuading or forcing labor unions and industry to abstain from attempts to raise their incomes, or at least to be more moderate.

Not everybody draws the appropriate conclusions from the theory which he espouses. And not everybody is willing to adopt policies to correct the undesirable situation. (Nor does everybody find the situation sufficiently undesirable to get seriously worried). The ambivalent position of many partisans of labor unions is noteworthy. They reject the wage-push diagnosis because, understandably, they do not wish to take the blame for the inflation. But they also reject the demand-pull diagnosis, because this diagnosis would militate against the use of fiscal and monetary policies to bolster employment.

They want effective demand to be increased at a rate fast enough to permit full employment at rapidly increasing wage rates; but they do not want to attribute increasing prices either to the increase in demand or to the increase in wage rates. The only way out of this logical squeeze is to blame the consumer-price increase on prices "administered" by big business; but in order to support this hypothesis one would have to prove that the profit margins and profit rates of the industries in question have been rising year after year — which they have not. But we shall see later that matters are not quite so simple and cannot be analyzed exclusively in these terms.

Our first task is to deal with the contention that the distinction between cost-push and demand-pull inflation is unworkable, irrelevant or even meaningless.

"Cost Push No Cause of Inflation"

There is a group of outstanding economists contending that there cannot be such a thing as a cost-push inflation because, without an increase in purchasing power and demand, cost increases would lead to unemployment and depression, not to inflation.

On their own terms, these economists are correct. The rules of inductive logic say that if A and B together cause M; and if A without B cannot cause M, whereas B without A can cause M; then B, and not A, should be called the cause of M. Make A the wage-raising power of the unions and the price-raising power of the corporations; make B the credit-creating and money-creating power of the monetary system; make M the successive price increases. It should be quite clear that without the creation of new purchasing power a continuing price increase would be impossible. Hold the amount of money and bank credit constant (relative to real national product) and all that the most powerful unions and corporations can do is to price themselves out of the market.

Having admitted all this to the economists who reject the possibility of cost-push inflation we can shift the weight of the argument to the question whether, given the power of the monetary system to create money and credit, the power would be exercised to the same extent if strong trade unions and strong corporations desisted from raising wages and prices as it actually is exercised when wages and prices are being pushed up. There would probably be quick agreement that, given our present system, the exercise of the wage-raising power of strong unions and the price-raising power of strong corporations induces, or adds impetus to, the exercise of the ability of the banking system to create purchasing power.

The point then is that an increase in effective demand is a necessary condition for a continuing increase in general prices, but that a cost-push under present conditions will regularly lead to an expansion of credit and to that increase in effective demand which will permit the increase in consumer prices.

There remains, however, an important question of fact. Assume it is decided not to exercise the power to create money and credit — more than is needed to maintain a constant ratio to real national product — even at the risk of severe unemployment that might result if wages and prices increased; would we then have to expect that the strong unions and corporations would continue to make use of their wage-raising and price-raising powers? Some economists are convinced that unions and business firms would adopt much more moderate policies if they had to fear that any lack of moderation would lead to unemployment and stagnation. This does not mean that a considerable level of unemployment would be required to impress industry and unions with the desirability of moderation. Industrial firms would know that, under an unyielding monetary policy, they could not hope to pass increases in labor cost on to consumers and they would therefore refuse to yield to union pressure. Unions, in turn, would not strike for higher wages if they were sure that industry could not afford to give in. Hence, no cost push and no extra unemployment.

Acceptance of this view by any number of economists would not yet make it a practicable policy. It could not work unless the monetary authorities embraced it without reservation, since any indication of a lack of faith and determination on the part of the authorities would remove the premise: unions could hope that industries would hope that an eventual relaxation of the monetary brake would "bail them out" and by means of an expansion of demand avert the business losses and the unemployment that would threaten to arise in consequence of wage and price increases.

"Demand Pull No Cause of Inflation"

Having shown that there is a sense in which the contention is correct that "cost push is no cause of inflation, it takes a demand pull to produce it," we shall now attempt to show that the opposite contention may likewise be correct. There are indeed assumptions for which it would be appropriate to say that "demand pull is no cause of inflation, it takes a cost push to produce it." What are these assumptions and how do they differ from those of the traditional model?

In the traditional model, prices rise or fall under the impact of anonymous market forces. They rise when at their existing level the quantity of goods demanded exceeds the quantity supplied. Not that producers, noticing the increased demand, would decide that they could do better if they "charged" more; rather the mechanism of a "perfect market" would automatically lift prices to the level where the consumers would not want to purchase any more than was supplied. Sellers, in this model, don't ask higher prices, they just get them. The same thing happens in the model of the perfect labor market. When the demand for labor increases, workers don't ask for higher wages, they just get them as a result of competition.

In a large part of our present economy, prices and wages do not "rise" as if lifted by the invisible hand, but are "raised" by formal and explicit managerial decisions. Assume now that prices and wage rates are administered everywhere in the economy in such a way that changes in demand are not taken into account; instead, they are set in accordance with some "rules of thumb." Prices and wages may then be so high (relative to demand) that inventories accumulate, production is cut, and labor is unemployed; or they may be so low (relative to demand) that inventories are depleted, production is raised, customers must patiently wait for delivery or their orders are rejected, and there are plenty of vacancies, but no workers to fill them. If the rules of thumb are universally observed by producers, distributors, and labor unions and take full account of increased cost of production and increased cost of living, but disregard all changes in demand, then there can be no demand pull upon prices. In such circumstances an increase in effective demand leads to unfilled orders and unfilled vacancies, but not to higher prices.[1]

One may object, of course, that such a model cannot possibly apply to all markets; that there exist numerous competitive markets in which no producer has enough power to "set" or "charge" a price; that in many markets in which prices are administered the would-be buyers, in periods of increased demand, offer higher prices in order to be served and sellers are glad to accept them even though they exceed their list prices; and that this regularly happens when the demand for labor is brisk, so that wages paid can be higher than the rates agreed in collective bargaining. Thus, demand pull is likely to work despite the existence of administered prices and wages.

Although the objection may be sustained on practical grounds,

---

[1] ". . . if all prices were administered on the basis of markup over direct cost — then excess demand might exist in all markets, yet without effect on the price level." Gardner Ackley, "Administered Prices and the Inflationary Process," *American Economic Review*, Papers and Proceedings, XLIX (May 1959), 421.

this does not destroy the value of the model. If there are, in actual fact, *many* industries where backlogs of orders accumulate while prices fail to rise and where job vacancies grow in number while wages fail to rise, then the model has some relevance, and it is legitimate to speculate about the functioning of an economic system in which *all* prices and wages are administered on the basis of cost calculations and held at the set levels even in the face of excess demand. It is not easy to decide whether on balance the institutions in our economy are such that a model featuring "market-clearing prices" or a model featuring "cost-plus prices" fits better the purposes of speculating about the over-all performance of the entire economy.

In any case, the contention must be granted that there may be conditions under which "effective demand" is not effective and won't pull up prices, and when it takes a cost push to produce price inflation. But this position disregards an important distinction, namely whether the cost push is "equilibrating" in the sense that it "absorbs" a previously existing excess demand or whether it is "disequilibrating" in the sense that it creates an excess supply (of labor and productive capacity) that will have to be prevented or removed by an increase in effective demand. Thus we are back at the crucial issue; a "monistic" interpretation cannot do justice to it.

Statistical Tests

It is possible to grant the usefulness of the distinction between cost push and demand pull in building theoretical models for speculative reasoning, and yet to deny its usefulness in identifying the causes of general price increases in concrete situations. It may be that the concepts are not operational, that statistical tests are either unavailable or unreliable.

Some have proposed to answer the question whether wage push or demand pull had "initiated" the upward movement of prices, by looking to see which has *increased first*, prices or wages. But "first" since what time? If prices and wages have risen in turn, in successive steps the choice of a base period is quite arbitrary and a conclusion assigning the leading or initiating role to one factor or the other would be equally arbitrary. (This is especially so if our statistical information is limited to annual data.)

Not much better is the idea of looking to see which of the two, money-wage rates or consumer prices, has *increased more*. The arbitrary choice of the base period for this comparison is again a serious difficulty. But even more important is the fact that the annual rise in productivity (output per labor hour) normally secures increases in real wages over the year. Hence it is to be expected that wage rates increase relative to consumer prices regardless of whether there is inflation, and regardless of whether prices are pulled up by demand or pushed up by wages.

Even some highly-seasoned economists have fallen victim to another logical snare: that any increase in money-wage rates that *exceeded the increase in labor productivity* was a sure sign of a wage push. Yet, even if there were not labor union in the country and no worker ever asked for higher wages, a demand-pull inflation would eventually pull up the wage level; and if the demand pull were such that prices and wages rose by any percentage above two or three a year — and it may well be five or ten or twenty per cent — money-wage rates would be up by more than the rate of increase in productivity. This, then, would have been the result of demand pull only, without any wage push at all. Hence the proposed statistical test is completely inconclusive.

A test which is based on a fundamentally correct chain of reasoning would compare profit rates with wage rates, and diagnose demand pull when *profit rates increase faster than wage rates*. A slight variant of this test uses the relative shares of profits and wages in national income. The theory behind these tests is simply this: when an expansion of effective demand — without a wage push — pulls up product prices, an increase in profits and profit rates would result until wage rates are pulled up by the derived demand for labor. On this theory, an increase in consumer prices associated with increased profit rates, but with wage rates lagging, would reliably indicate the existence of a demand-pull inflation. The operational difficulties with a test based on this theory are the same as those connected with other statistical tests: the arbitrary selection of the time periods. The theory, moreover, applies to an economy in which most prices are the result of anonymous market forces, not of administrative decisions. If most prices were administered and the price setters decided to raise their "profit targets" (perhaps at the same time that trade unions were out to engineer a wage boost, but a little faster or by a bigger jump) we could find — given the present monetary regime guided by the high-level-employment goal — that prices and profit rates increase ahead of wage rates even though the movement was not started by an autonomous expansion of demand. Hence, the lead of profit rates is not a reliable indication of demand pull; it may occur also in conjunction with a cost push in which price setters take a leading part.

Widely accepted as reliable symptoms of demand-pull inflation are over-employment and over-time payments. The statistical operations proposed to establish these symptoms are, for over-employment, to see whether *job vacancies exceed job applications* and, for over-time pay, to see whether *average hourly earnings have increased faster than wage rates*. Some critics rightly point out that the presence of these symptoms does not rule out that some cost push has contributed to the inflation of prices. Indeed it would have been possible that a cost push actually initiated the process and that the compensatory monetary injection, expanding demand to avoid the threatening un-employment, turned out to be heavier than necessary. Thus while these tests can verify the existence of an inflation of demand, they cannot prove that it was excess demand that precipitated the inflation of consumer prices.

PROPOSED CONCEPTS AND DISTINCTIONS

The diversity of expert opinion and the absence of any good statistical tests to support a diagnosis may in part be due to the lack of precise definitions. It is clear that an inflation of effective demand is a nec-essary condition not only for a demand-pull inflation of consumer prices but also for a cost-push inflation. Without an expansion of demand the cost boost would result in less production and less em-ployment, not in a continuing rise of the level of consumer prices. Should one then speak of a demand-pull inflation only when the expansion in demand is clearly the initiating factor and any adminis-trative cost increases are clearly induced? Or should one also speak of a demand-pull inflation if administrative wage and material-price increases start and lead the procession of events, but are then joined and overtaken by induced or compensatory expansions of demand?

Autonomous, Induced, and Supportive Demand Inflation

It is useful to distinguish autonomous from induced and supportive expansions of demand. *Autonomous* would be expansions which are not linked to previous or to expected cost increases; hence, disburse-ments which would also occur if no cost increases had been experi-enced or anticipated. *Induced* expansions of demand are direct con-sequences of a cost increase, in that those who receive the increased cost-prices or those who pay them will make larger disbursements than they would have made otherwise. For example, the industrial firms yielding to union pressure for a wage increase may borrow from banks (or dig into cash reserves) in order to pay the higher wage bill; or the recipients of higher wages may increase installment purchases and induce an expansion of consumer credit. *Supportive* (compensatory) expansions of demand would be those which are engineered by monetary or fiscal policy designed to reduce the unemployment arising, or threatening to arise, from cost increases. For example, the monetary authorities may reduce reserve requirements or create reserves in order to allow banks to extend loans, or the fiscal authorities may increase government expenditures in an attempt to expand effective demand and employment.

Without wishing to restrict the freedom of choice of those who formulate definitions, I submit that the choice should be appropriate to the purposes for which the concept is used. If the concept of a demand-induced inflation, or demand-pull inflation, is to serve for diagnostic and prognostic purposes in the development of economic policies, it would seem preferable to confine it to autonomous expansions of demand. This would not obstruct but rather aid the analysis of instances in which cost-induced expansions or supportive expansions of demand should turn out to be excessive in the sense that they create more employment opportunities than are destroyed by the cost increases, and hence give rise to some of the symptoms of a demand-induced inflation.

Aggressive, Defensive, and Responsive Cost Inflation

Similar obscurities due to a lack of essential distinctions surround the concept of the cost-induced inflation. Perhaps so much is clear that the term refers to increases in consumer prices that are the (direct or indirect) result of cost increases — labor cost, material cost, or any other cost. But it is not clear whether these cost increases have to be *autonomous* in the sense that they would not have come about in the absence of any monopoly power (price-making power), merely as a result of competitive demand. For it is quite possible that formal administrative decisions are behind cost increases which, however, do not go beyond what would have occurred without such decisions. For example, a trade union may achieve a "victory" in its negotiations with an employer group bringing home the same raise in pay which the individual employers would have offered (without collective bargaining) in trying to get or keep the labor force they want. Let us decide to call these cost increases *responsive* (or competitive) to distinguish them from those that could *not* be obtained in a purely competitive market.

It would be misleading to denote all non-responsive (non-competitive) price or wage increases as "autonomous," since they may well be "induced" by some changes in the economic situation. And the adjectives "autonomous" and "induced" are usually used as opposites. A wage-rate increase, for example, is not responsive unless it is in response to an excess demand (short supply) in the particular labor market; but an increase which is not "demand-induced" (and which therefore presupposes some "autonomy" with respect to competitive market forces) may yet be induced by (a) an increase in the employer's profits, (b) an increase in wage rates obtained by other labor groups, or (c) an increase in the cost of living. I propose to call (a) a "profit-induced" wage increase, (b) an "imitative" (or "spill-over", wage increase, and (c) a "defensive" wage increase. Any one of these increases may act as either an "impulse" or a "propagation" factor in the inflationary process.

Profit-induced and imitative increases as well as spontaneous increases may be called *aggressive* because they are designed to achieve a new advance in the real wage rate. A *defensive* increase merely restores real earnings which the group in question has long been enjoying; an aggressive increase raises real earnings above that level. The specification of a time interval is necessary in the definition so that one avoids calling "defensive" what really is a battle to defend the ground just gained in an aggressive action. For example, an aggressive wage-rate increase of ten per cent is likely to be partially eroded within less than a year through the resulting cost-push inflation (aided by induced and supportive expansions of demand). If the same trade unions then demand "cost-of-living raises" to restore their real wages, it would be somewhat ironic to call these new wage adjustments "defensive." But there will always be a wide range in which cost increases may as legitimately be considered defensive as aggressive, especially since trade unions take turns in their actions, each defending the real earnings of its own members that have suffered in consequence of the aggressive actions of other unions, and at the same time attempting to obtain a net improvement.

Administrative price increases by industries producing materials and other producers goods which enter as significant cost items into the prices of many other products can likewise be characterized as responsive (competitive), defensive, or aggressive. Purely responsive increases cannot occur in an industry with much unused productive capacity; only when plants are working at capacity and orders are piling up can administrative price increases be merely responsive; in such circumstances it is economically irrelevant that these prices are administered. Defensive increases leave real profit rates substantially unchanged; these increases take account of increased production cost and no more. Needless to say, the rates of return must be calculated on the basis of the reproduction cost of the required capacity;

that is to say, the book values of the fixed capital may be too low if reproduction cost of buildings and equipment is higher than at the time of their acquisition, or too high if assets are included which are not required for current production. Thus, price increases designed to defend, in periods of falling production, a profit rate that is calculated on the basis of the value of assets inclusive of unused capacity are really aggressive; and price increases designed to raise the money rate of return on capital just enough to take care of increased replacement costs are really defensive.

Should all kinds of wage increase and price increase be included in the concept of a cost-push inflation whenever they are collectively negotiated, unilaterally announced, or otherwise the result of administrative action? I submit that increases which are merely responsive (competitive) do not belong there at all. Defensive increases do of course play an important role in the process of price inflation and the economist will surely not leave them out of his analysis. But in an explanation of an inflationary process going on year-in year-out the aggressive increases have a more substantive role to play than defensive increases; and when it comes to assign "blame" for an inflation of consumer prices, the aggressive cost boosts will obviously be the more eligible candidates.

The Basic Model Sequences

With the help of the proposed concepts the two basic model sequences of consumer-price inflation can be easily described.

(A) *Demand-pull infla-tion:*	Autonomous expansions of demand (government spending, business spending, consumer spending) are followed by responsive (competitive) price and wage increases.
(B) *Cost-push infla-tion:*	Aggressive increases of wage rates and/or material prices are followed by induced and/or supportive (compensatory) demand expansions.

Cost-push models are relatively simple as long as they contain only a single impulse — either wage or price increases — with all sequential changes in the nature of adjustments.

(B-1) *"Pure" wage-push inflation:*	Aggressive increases of wage rates are followed by induced and/or supportive demand expansions, and by responsive increases of material prices and other wage rates.

(B-2) *"Pure" price-push inflation:* Aggressive increases of material prices are followed by induced and/or supportive demand expansions, and by responsive increases of other materials prices and wage rates.

Models become more complicated as more discretionary actions are included in the sequence of events, especially imitative and defensive increases of cost elements, or even aggressive increases, requiring further adjustments. For example, an autonomous demand expansion may be followed by administered wage and price increases more drastic than merely competitive increases would be; thus, the increases would be partly responsive and partly aggressive, requiring further demand expansions, induced or supportive, if unemployment is to be avoided. Or, aggressive wage and price increases may be followed by excessive demand expansions, perhaps because a nervous government rushes in with overdoses of supportive injections of buying power; some of the effective demand thus created would then be in the nature of an autonomous expansion, resulting in further (responsive) upward adjustments of costs.

ATTEMPTED APPLICATION

Even the most complicated model sequence will probably still be much simpler than the actual course of events as reflected in the data at our disposal. Since reality is so messy that no neat and simple model will fit at all closely, whereas various complex models will fit approximately, it is not surprising that even impartial analysts arrive at divergent interpretations of the so-called facts.

The Postwar Inflation

In the narrow scope of this article no attempt can be made to sift the data, to assess the comparative applicability of the various models, and to award first prize to the best-fitting model. But I shall not dodge this question and shall indicate briefly what impressions I have derived from the data presented by governmental and private researchers.

I believe that for an explanation of the consumer-price inflation from 1945 to 1948, and from 1950 to 1952, the basic model of the demand-pull inflation does as well as, or better than, any of the other models, simple or complicated. On the other hand, for the period 1955–59 several cost-push models appear to do better, and I am prepared to regard the consumer-price increases of these four years as a result of a cost-push inflation.

The choice among the various cost-push models is a hard one, especially in view of the controversy about the behavior of administered material prices. The periodic increases in steel prices have sometimes been regarded as the most strategic impulse factor in the inflationary process. A special theory of "profit-target pricing" assuming "periodic raising of the target" has been devised in support of this diagnosis and an array of empirical material has been added in its support.

Wage or Profit Push?

Neither this theory nor the statistical data seem to me to make the model of the "material-price-push inflation" a plausible explanation of the period in question. While many of the administered price increases may have hampered the performance of our economy and accelerated the inflationary process, I doubt that all or most of them have been "aggressive" in the sense defined. The reported data on profit rates and profit margins do not, in my judgment, indicate that the price increases were aggressive. Of course, few, if any, of the increases since 1955 have been in the nature of responsive adjustments to excess demand — but probably most of them were defensive in nature, taking account of cost increases without raising real profit rates. I cannot verify this impression of mine to everybody's satisfaction, and perhaps not even to my own. But my impression is strengthened by the deduced consequences of certain assumptions which I consider plausible, concerning the policies and objectives of business managers.

There is, in my opinion, nothing invidious in contending that there are essential differences between most wage increases obtained by strong labor unions and most increases of material prices announced by strong corporations. Nor it is meant to be critical of union policies or uncritical of business policies if many wage increases are held to be aggressive, and many administered price increases defensive. The point is that the situation of most businesses is such that a series of aggressive price increases would be either injurious to them in the long run or downright impossible. A series of aggressive wage increases, on the other hand, may be both possible and beneficial to the labor groups concerned.

To hold that most administered price increases have been defensive rather than aggressive, does not mean (a) that the prices in question were not too high — they probably were, (b) that the increases did not speed up the inflationary process — they certainly did, or (c) that they were "justified" — which they were not if a competitive market model is used as the standard. But if the question is only whether these price increases were the "impulse factors," the "initiating forces" of the price inflation, then I believe the answer is negative.

WAGE INCREASES AND PRODUCTIVITY

I do not expect serious exception to the proposition that most of the wage increases obtained by strong trade unions in the last four years, whether spontaneous or profit-induced or imitative, have been aggressive in the sense defined. (This is in contrast to most wage increases between 1945 and 1952, which were responsive.) We must now inquire whether aggressive wage increases are inflationary if they do not exceed the relative rate at which productivity increases.

Aggressive Wage Increases to Capture Average Productivity Gains

According to accepted doctrine, the consumer price level can be held approximately stable, and full employment maintained, if the average increase in money-wage rates does not exceed the average increase in productivity in the economy as a whole. Some of the necessary qualifications to this proposition are not relevant to the issues under discussion. For interested readers they are presented in a footnote.[2] One qualification, however, that may matter here to some extent

---

[2] There is first the qualification for the sacrifice of fixed-income recipients. The existence of contractual payments in fixed money amounts makes it possible for wage rates to increase a little more than productivity. Assume, for the sake of a simple arithmetical illustration, that of a national product of $1000 a share of $700 is distributed in the form of wages, $100 in the form of profits, and $200 in the form of fixed interest, rent, and pension payments. If now net national product rises by $20 (or 2 per cent) and the recipients of fixed money incomes get no share in the increased product (because prices are held stable), 20 per cent of the increased product, i.e., $4, becomes available as a possible bonus for labor in addition to their 70 per cent share or $14. Total wage payments can thus increase by $18 or 2.57 per cent.

A second qualification relates to possible improvements in the terms of trade. Assume that the price of imports (relative to the price of exports) falls by 2 per cent and that imports had amounted to 10 per cent of the net national product, or $100. If the entire gain of $2 is seized as another bonus for labor, wages can rise by $20 or 2.86 per cent.

A third qualification concerns the possible effects of increased tax revenues. Assume that the effective tax rate on profits (distributed plus undistributed) is 50 per cent while the marginal tax rate on wages is 20 per cent. The additional profits are (10 per cent of $20 =) $2 and the taxes on this are $1. The taxes on additional wages are (20 per cent of $20 =) $4. If the government kept expenditures constant despite increased revenues, another bonus of $5 could be distributed in the form of wages, bringing the total addition to $25

concerns the additional profits needed as returns on the additional investments required for the increase in national product. It is sometimes possible for total product per worker to increase thanks to a progress of technology, organization, or skills, without any increase in capital investment. More often, however, it takes some additional investment to achieve an increase in productivity. If such investments were not allowed to earn a return, progress might be stopped short; but if they are to earn a return, total profits must increase lest the rates of return on capital are cut, which could lead to reduced investment and employment. Hence, as a rule, wage increases must not absorb the entire increase in output. And if the additional investment were so large that capital per worker has increased at a percentage rate greater than that of output per worker, wage rates cannot even increase by as much as output per worker and still allow price stability with full employment.[3]

The following formulation will steer clear of such technicalities and express the essential points. Apart from a few modifying influences, such as a squeezing of quasi-rents in stagnant industries, a whittling down of the real claims of recipients of contractual incomes, or a lucky improvement in the terms of foreign trade, real wages per worker cannot increase faster than product per worker. If *money*-wage rates are raised faster than productivity, and the monetary authorities supply the money needed to pay the increased wages without unemployment, prices will rise enough to keep *real*-wage rates from rising faster than productivity. To say that the price inflation has the

---

before taxes, or more than the entire increase in net national product. (We neglect now the tax on the third bonus.) Wages before taxes could with all three bonuses be increased by 3.57 per cent, compared with a 2 per cent increase in national income.

The second and third bonuses, however, cannot be counted upon; the second bonus may just as likely be negative since the terms of trade may deteriorate rather than improve. Even the first bonus is likely to disappear in an economy with perpetual inflation, because contractual incomes might gradually be made subject to automatic cost-of-living adjustments. All three qualifications are probably less important than the one presented in the text and this one works in the opposite direction.

This exposition has been freely adapted from Friedrich A. Lutz, "Cost- and Demand-Induced Inflation," *Banca Nazionale del Lavoro*, No. 44 (March 1958), 9–10. The adaptations were necessary because I believe Lutz's argument to be partly erroneous.

[3] If wage rates were to increase as much as output per worker while prices were kept from rising, total output would not be large enough to allow any return to be earned by the new capital; employers, then, might not want to maintain the level of investment and employment. See Lutz, *loc. cit.*, 4.

"function" of keeping the increase in real wages down to the rate at which productivity increases may help some to understand the mechanism. But it is not really an appropriate expression, for nothing has to "function" to "prevent from occurring" what cannot occur anyway. Either prices rise (with the help of supportive expansion of demand) to cut the real wage rates to the level made possible by the productivity increase, or unemployment occurs (if demand expansion is prevented or restrained) and cuts total real wages even lower.

If money wages were not increased at all and all increments to the net national product that are due to technological progress were distributed to consumers in the form of lower prices, *all* income recipients — wage earners, owners of businesses, and fixed-income recipients — would share in the increased product. If money wages all over the economy are increased approximately by the rate at which average productivity has increased, prices on the average will neither fall nor rise and hence the fixed-income recipients (bondholders, landlords, pensioners, perhaps also civil servants, teachers, etc.) will be cut out of their share in the increment. Thus, aggressive money wage increases which, on the average, equal the average increase in productivity in the economy will improve the relative income share of labor at the expense of the receivers of contractual income.

Aggressive Wage Increases to Capture Individual Productivity Gains

The "rule" that price stability and full employment can be maintained if all money wage rates are increased by the same percentage by which average productivity has increased in the economy as a whole is frequently misunderstood and mistakenly applied to advocate increases in money-wage rates in individual firms or industries by the same percentage by which productivity has increased in these firms or industries. In other words, the rule is perverted to the proposal that the benefits of advancing productivity should accrue to the workers in the industries in which the advances take place. It is twisted into a proposition justifying

. . . union demands in those industries, which, because of improved technology and consequent cost reductions can afford to pay higher wages without charging higher prices for their products. This proposition is thoroughly unsound. It misses completely the economic function of prices and wages; its realization would sabotage the economic allocation of resources without serving any purpose that could be justified from any ethical or political point of view.[4]

[4] Fritz Machlup, *The Political Economy of Monopoly* (Baltimore, 1952), 403.

A sensible allocation of resources requires that the same factors of production are offered at the same prices to all industries. It causes misallocations if industries in which technology has improved are forced to pay higher wages for the same type of labor that gets lower pay in industries where technology has not changed. Wage rates should be temporarily higher in fields into which labor is to be attracted, not in fields where labor is released by labor-saving techniques. It is economic nonsense to advocate that wage rates should be forced up precisely where labor becomes relatively abundant.

One might accept an economically unsound arrangement if it were ethically much superior. But no one could claim that the proposition in question satisfied any ethical norm. If five industries, let us call them A, B, C, D, and E, employ the same type of labor; if any of them, say Industry A, develops a new production process and is now able to make the same product as before with half the amount of labor; then this Industry A could afford to raise its wage rates without raising its selling prices. Should now workers in Industry A get a wage increase of 100 per cent while their fellow workers in Industries B, C, D, and E get nothing? Should the coincidence that the technological advance took place in A give the workers there the windfall of the entire benefit, raising them above the rest of the people? I can see no ethical argument that could be made in favor of such a scheme.

But as a matter of practical fact, apart from economics and ethics, the scheme could never be consistently applied, because the workers in other industries would not stand for it, . . . similar wage increases would have to be given in all . . . firms and industries regardless of their ability to pay, regardless of whether their selling prices would remain stable or go up slightly or a great deal. It simply would not be fair if a favored group were to be the sole beneficiary of progress while the rest of the population would have to sit back and wait for better luck.[5]

No fair-minded person would ask them to sit back and wait; every labor union with any power at all would press the claims of its members, and where no unions existed workers would eventually appeal to their employers and to the public to end the injustice. Yet, any "equalizing" wage increases would be clearly of the cost-push type and would, if unemployment is prevented, lead to consumer price increases which take away from the originally privileged worker groups some of the real gains they were first awarded (with the approval of short-sighted commentators and politicians).

This spill-over of money-wage increases and the cost-push inflation which it produces (with the help of a supportive demand infla-

[5] *Ibid.*, 404–405.

tion) serve to redistribute some of the productivity gains first captured by the workers in the industries where the gains occurred. This redistribution by means of consumer-price inflation cuts back the real wages of the first-successful labor groups, whose unions will then complain about the erosion of their incomes and will call for seemingly defensive wage increases to regain the ground lost through inflation (though they rarely lose all of their gain in real income and often keep a large part of it).

In short, a policy that condones wage increases in industries which, because of increased productivity, can afford to pay increased wages without charging increased prices, is actually a policy that accepts a rising cost-price spiral without end.

PRICE REDUCTIONS ESSENTIAL FOR STABILITY

A wage increase obtained by a particular labor group may initiate an inflationary process, but the speed of this process will depend largely on the incidence of defensive price increases and of imitative and defensive wage increases. If nothing but responsive (competitive) price and wage increases were to occur, the rate of inflation initiated by an isolated wage boost would be very small, perhaps negligible. It is, nevertheless, interesting to examine models of price inflation that include neither defensive nor imitative increases.

Inflation Without Spill-Over Wage Push

In the inflationary process described in the last section, the industries that were forced to pay the increased wages (out of the economies provided by improved techniques) were assumed for the sake of the argument not to increase their selling prices. The price inflation was chiefly the work of a spill-over of the wage increases into fields where productivity had increased less or not at all. But even in the absence of any spill-over, even if no worker in the country were to receive a raise that did not come from economies in production, some degree of consumer-price inflation would be inevitable in an economy in which (a) wage rates are never reduced in any sector, even in the face of unemployment, (b) wage rates are increased to capture productivity gains entirely in the industries where they accrue, and (c) full employment is secured, if necessary, through expansion of effective demand. Now when workers are released in the industries where productivity increases, but production, with unchanged prices and unchanged demand, is not increased, it will take an inflation of demand to create employment for the workers set free by the advance of technology. In other words, the "technological unemployment" will have to be cured by an expansion of demand, which in turn will cause a rise in consumer prices.

Does not this argument overlook the increase in demand on the part of workers who receive wage increases? It does not. Since the wage increases were granted just to offset the cost reduction made possible by the increase in output per worker, the workers who stay employed receive their raise out of funds no longer paid out as wages to the workers who lost their jobs. A little arithmetic may clarify this point. If 90 workers can now produce the output previously produced by 100, and are now paid the total wage that was previously paid to 100, the total purchasing power in the hands of the workers stays the same. The 10 workers who were released get nothing, and what was saved on them is being paid to the "more productive" 90. The firm, paying the same wage bill (though to fewer workers), finds its costs neither increased nor reduced and keeps its selling prices unchanged. Since at these prices demand is the same as before, the firm has no use for the 10 workers; nor has anybody else if wages rates are nowhere reduced. If the authorities want them reemployed, a demand inflation has to be engineered. True, the 10 workers will produce something once they are employed, but only after increased prices have created incentives for employers to use more labor; or they will have to be employed (and paid for with new money) in the production of public services not sold in the market.

The assumptions built into the model underlying this chain of reasoning have excluded growth (of labor force and capital stock) and excess capacity. If there were adequate excess capacity in each and every line of production, the demand created (in order to reemploy the labor released by the more productive industries) could be satisfied without price increases anywhere. But no inflation model can reasonably include the assumption of ubiquitous excess capacity; limited facilities (bottlenecks) are implied in any explanation of inflation. Thus, no exception should be taken to the assumption that the new wages paid to the reemployed workers will not all be spent for their own products, but largely for other things, and that prices will be bid up in the process.

The exclusion of a growing labor force and a growing capital stock have served merely to simplify the reasoning. When inputs and outputs are increasing, a certain increase in the money supply and in aggregate spending will be required to manage the increase in output and trade at given prices. An expansion of money demand to effect a re-absorption of technological unemployment would be over and above the money demand required to take care of the growth in labor force and capital stock. To combine the analyses of such growth and of technological unemployment would be an unnecessary complication; the other growth factors can be disregarded without vitiating the conclusions derived in an isolated treatment of technological unemployment.

The price inflation to be expected from a demand inflation engineered to absorb "technological unemployment" will of course be quite moderate in this case, where all the spill-over wage increases are ruled out. Here is a type of inflation that cannot be characterized as a cost-push inflation, and not as a demand-pull inflation either, if that term is reserved for autonomous expansions of demand. To be sure, aggressive wage increases are involved in the process, but these increases, merely offsetting the growth of productivity, will push up only the cost per labor hour, not the cost per unit of output, and thus no price increases can be said to result from cost increases.

Inflation Without Any Wage Increases

One may easily jump to the conclusion that technological unemployment, and the need to resort to demand inflation as its only cure, is entirely due to the aggressive wage increases giving to the workers in the technically advancing industries the entire benefit of the productivity gain. This conclusion would be wrong. The consequences will be the same if in the absence of any wage increase the firms in question find their profits increased but for some reason fail to let consumers benefit in the form of lower selling prices.

Does this argument rely on lower marginal propensities to spend, or on insufficient investment opportunities, or on excessive liquidity preferences? It does not. Even if it is assumed that corporations spend all of their retained profits and stockholders spend all their dividends — just as the workers would have spent their wages — the workers released in the industries where technology has advanced will not be re-employed without the help of demand inflation unless prices to consumers are lowered. The case is almost the same as that in which the workers captured the productivity gain, except that now the corporations and their owners pocket the entire benefit.

Why "almost" the same, why not exactly the same? Because there is the possibility that an increase in retained earnings, as an increase in capital supply, raises the marginal productivity of labor and thus the demand for labor at given wage rates. But it would be absurd to expect that this would suffice to re-employ all the released labor. Assume that the entire amount saved on the wage bill is spent on new machinery; this new demand for machinery (and indirectly for the labor that goes into its manufacture) merely takes the place of the former workers' demand for consumer goods (and indirectly for the labor that went into their production). Thus the spending of the retained profits — earned by reducing the wage bill — constitutes no increased demand for labor. Only the resulting increase in productive facilities may eventually help the demand for labor to the extent of a small fraction of the technological unemployment created by the (labor-saving) increase in productivity. Hence the conclusion is the same as it was in the case of wage increase: only if consumers get a chance through lower prices to buy more product with their given money incomes will the released workers get a chance to find jobs in the absence of demand inflation.[6]

But why should firms refuse to lower their prices when production costs fall? The well-known theoretical models of a monopolist responding to a lowering of his cost curve show with no reasonable exceptions that he would reduce his selling price and increase his output. If firms can be observed acting otherwise, what is wrong with the model or what is wrong with the firms? One possible hypothesis would be that the firms of the real world had been in "disequilibrium," charging less than profit-maximizing monopoly prices and waiting for a good occasion to adjust their position. If now their costs are reduced, inaction, failure to reduce their prices, may be an easy way to adjust. Another hypothesis would be that the firms of the real world are in positions of not firmly coordinated oligopoly, where the safest rule is always "not to rock the boat," that is, never to reduce prices lest a rival mistake it for an outbreak of price competition. A third hypothesis would be that the "administered" prices in modern business cannot be explained by any models based on intelligent considerations, but are set by some fixed rules of thumb, and that one of these rules is never to reduce a price. There are perhaps still other hypotheses to explain the fact of "downward inflexibility" of prices — if indeed it is a fact. But no matter which hypothesis is accepted, the conclusion remains valid that if prices are not reduced when produc-

---

[6] This does not mean that the entire increase in productivity must be passed on to consumers in the form of reduced prices. Technological unemployment will neither be perpetuated nor require a price-inflating demand expansion for its cure if wage rates are raised by the national average increase in productivity. This will still permit price reductions in the industries where productivity has increased. The money the consumers save in buying these products at reduced prices will be spent on other goods and will drive up some other prices, without however raising consumer prices on the average.

tivity has increased, technological unemployment arises and cannot be absorbed except through demand inflation and consequent consumer-price inflation.

Stabilization of Individual Prices Necessitates Inflation

The argument of the preceding pages was designed to demonstrate that the failure to reduce prices in industries where productivity has increased will result in an inflationary increase of general prices, which

(a) will be most rapid if the productivity gains are captured by the workers of these industries by way of wage rate increases — because of the practically inevitable spill-over of the wage increases to other worker groups; but

(b) will also occur, though much more slowly, in the absence of such spill-over, because it will take a demand expansion to re-employ the workers released when the wage bill of the progressive industries is distributed over fewer workers; and

(c) will not be avoided even in the absence of any wage increases, because a demand expansion will be required to re-employ the workers released when the entire part of the wage bill that is saved through the technological advance is transformed into profits without giving consumers a chance to buy more product.

An economist willing to rely on the most abstract and general principles of economic theory can derive this "inevitability" of inflation from a simple set of theorems. He can deduce from the equilibrium conditions in a system of general equilibrium that general prices must rise if individual prices are maintained in industries where productivity increases. For a fall of production cost in one industry will call forth a reduction of the price of its product relative to the prices of all other products; this adjustment of relative prices will, in a money economy, proceed either through a fall in the money price of the product that now requires less labor per unit than before or through an increase in all other money prices (or through a combination of both); hence, stabilization of the money price of the more economically produced product implies that equilibrium will be restored through a general increase in money prices.

I do not propose to use this technical way of reasoning to convince trade union leaders, business executives, or members of Congress. But the previous argument was, I trust, understandable before I added the sophisticated demonstration of its conclusion.

The O'Mahoney Plan to Check Inflation

It should now be clear that the only way to prevent inflation of consumer prices, and prevent unemployment too, is to make prices more flexible in the downward direction and, in particular, to encourage price reductions in industries where productivity has increased. Senator O'Mahoney's plan, partly incorporated in Senate Bill 215 of April 1959, and receiving serious consideration by several members of Congress, would achieve exactly the opposite. According to the preamble of the Bill, its author believes that "inflation will be checked if the pricing policies of these [dominant] corporations are publicly reviewed before increased prices may be made effective." On this theory the Bill provides for public hearings and investigations of large corporations whenever they want to raise prices. But the harder it is made for firms to raise prices the more surely will they avoid ever reducing their prices.

If a nation is committed to a full-employment policy, that is, to a policy of using demand inflation to create employment, it can avoid inflation only by avoiding anything that may create unemployment. Since economic growth proceeds chiefly through technological progress, and technological unemployment can only be avoided through price reductions, the prime requirement of a non-inflationary full-employment policy is to prevent the workers, owners, and managers of the progressing industries from capturing all the productivity gains accruing in these industries in the form of increased money wages and increased profits, respectively, and to encourage the dispersion of most of these gains to consumers in the form of reduced prices.

The O'Mahoney policy in effect encourages the trade unions in the industries in question to get out and capture the entire productivity gains for their workers. It does so implicitly because, if the firms are prevented from raising prices after the aggressive wage increases have absorbed "only" the new economies, the labor unions will no longer be blamed by the public for causing or precipitating higher prices. The "visible link" between these wage increases and price inflation is removed, and the union leaders will have even less compunction in pressing for these supposedly non-inflationary wage increases. The firms, losing all or most of the productivity gains to their workers, will hardly be eager to reduce prices. But even if they should, by means of tough bargaining, succeed in keeping a good deal of the gains, they will surely not dream of sharing any part of them with the consumers, because they would consider it foolish to reduce prices that cannot be raised again except after expensive, cumbersome, and perhaps embarrassing public inquisitions.

The O'Mahoney plan to check inflation would actually tend to make inflation perennial and perpetual. The only thing that can be said for the proposed policy is that it might in the short run, perhaps for a couple of years, slow down the progress of the price inflation. But even this is doubtful since, apart from encouraging trade unions to fight for the productivity gains accruing in their industries, it does nothing to check the spill-over wage increases, which in genuine cost-push fashion engender many chains of defensive, "approvable" price increases and necessitate continual resort to supportive demand inflation.

CONCLUSION

It was not the purpose of this article to lead up to a critique of a proposed policy; this was a mere by-product. The intention was to examine the conceptual framework employed in recent discussions and, in view of its inadequacies, to propose some improved theoretical tools that may serve better in the analysis of the inflationary process of our time.

Analysis requires the following distinctions: an administered cost increase may be "equilibrating" in the sense that it merely "absorbs" a previously existing excess demand, or it may be "disequilibrating" in the sense that it creates an excess supply that may be prevented or removed only by an expansion of demand. To facilitate the analysis, three kinds of demand expansion are distinguished: *autonomous, induced* and *supportive*. Likewise three kinds of cost increase are distinguished: *responsive, defensive,* and *aggressive*. Any one of these cost increases may be "administered"; but the responsive ones would also occur in a fully competitive market. Neither defensive nor aggressive increases are in response to excess demand, and both therefore presuppose monopolistic power; defensive increases, however, attempt merely to restore previous real earnings of the group concerned, while aggressive increases raise real earnings above previous levels.

With the aid of these new concepts one can construct models of the inflationary process of various degrees of complexity. It may be possible to develop empirical tests for the choice of the model that fits best the recorded data of particular periods. The author believes that the price inflations of the periods 1945-48 and 1950-52 were of the demand-pull type, but that for 1955-59 a cost-push model would fit better. He tentatively suggests that wage push was more effective than profit push.

Finally the relation of inflation to increases in productivity was examined. The popular idea of a "non-inflationary" distribution of productivity gains by way of wage increases to the workers employed in the industries in which technology has advanced was found to be untenable. Imitative wage increases would lead to a brisk inflation. But some degree of inflation would occur even without such "spill-over" wage increases, because the distribution of the productivity gains to the workers or owners in the progressing industries would result in technological unemployment, and remedial full-employment measures would inflate the price level. The only way of avoiding inflation is through price reductions in industries where productivity has improved.

PART FOUR

INFLATION AND ECONOMIC CHANGE

WILLARD L. THORP AND RICHARD E. QUANDT

Growth, Productivity, and Inflation*

In their discussion of the relationship between productivity and inflation, Thorp and Quandt disagree with Machlup's contention that inflation necessarily results when productivity gains are accompanied by
increased factor returns rather than by lower prices. Although they
agree with Machlup that "the economy does not move by aggregates," they invoke macroeconomic reasoning in criticizing a policy
of increasing wages in individual industries on the basis of national
productivity gains.

Thorp and Quandt do not criticize such a policy on the grounds
that it is inherently inflationary. They do not consider moderate inflation a one-sided economic evil. In their view of economic growth the
primary engine of growth is increased investment, and the major determinant of the level of investment is the relationship between the rate
of profit and the rate of interest. They hold that inflation tends to
widen the gap between profit rates and interest rates and thus leads
to increased investment and, consequently, to economic growth.

*From Willard L. Thorp and Richard E. Quandt, *The New Inflation* (New
York, 1959), pp. 99–129. Reprinted by permission of McGraw-Hill Book
Company.

According to this argument, a demand-pull inflation raises prices more than costs, thus increasing profits and initiating the investment growth process. Even under a cost-push inflation profit rates increase because when prices rise in response to increased costs, they tend to increase at the same percentage rate as the cost rise, thus raising money profits. Furthermore, in any type of inflation, profit rates increase because money profits rise while the cost (value) of existing capital reflects the lower prices of an earlier period.

While the profit rate rises during an inflation, interest rates also tend to increase as savers switch from fixed obligations to more volatile common stocks. An equilibrium is reached between rising stock prices and lower bond prices (higher interest rates) at a point which yields a wider spread between profit and interest rates than existed prior to the inflation.

On the surface it would appear that the sharper and stronger the inflation, the greater the stimulus to economic growth. Thorp and Quandt argue, however, that a severe inflation would disrupt the economic system and would direct funds to speculative rather than productive areas.

The validity of their belief in the salutary effects of moderate inflation hinges on the concept of profit followed by businessmen in their investment decisions. While it might be true that inflation increases current money profits, and profit rates related to existing capital, there is some question as to the importance of current profits in investment decisions. In evaluating the profitability of an intended investment, the businessman might be in an optimistic frame of mind because of his firm's current prosperity, but the crucial elements in his decision whether or not to invest are the relationship between gross returns on the investment, the costs of undertaking and maintaining the investment, and current and future interest rates. Of course, if he expects an existing inflation to continue indefinitely he will be stimulated to invest. However, if he does not expect prices to rise or fall, the fact that his current profit rate is high because his money profits related to past investment (present capital) have increased, will have no effect on his estimate of the profitability of the new investment, which must be undertaken at current, high, prices. If he makes any reference to past experience, he will realize that inflationary periods have almost always been of much shorter duration than the life span of the average investment project. Thus, the positive effect of inflation on investment is negligible. Its role is limited to those instances where inflation is regarded as a continued rather than a temporary phenomenon; and even then, its contribution is but one of the influences, direct and indirect, bearing on the investment decision.

SOME of the comments about inflation in the earlier chapters may have made it seem that rising incomes and inflation are synonymous. So far as the United States is concerned, this is far from the truth. Incomes have been rising but so has production. On a per capita basis, the average individual's personal consumption expenditure increased from $497 in 1948 to $1,670 in 1958 or by 234 per cent. If these figures are put in terms of 1958 dollars so that they represent a *real* improvement, then the increase has been from $1,016 to $1,670 or 64 per cent. The difference between the 64 per cent and the 234 per cent is the part contributed by rising prices.

There can be no argument that the significant measure of welfare of the community is not the dollar value of output but the actual or real volume of goods and services which are made available to the consumer. Higher prices do not mean added real income. In these terms, even new factories and new equipment are not important in themselves but only as they can be expected to contribute to the capacity for meeting more of the demands of consumers.

The real growth in the economy may come from various sources — more labor and capital, better organization, a shift in the composition of output to products where more output comes from less input, and technological progress. In economic terms, real growth means that more goods and services will be available. When this has been achieved through any of the above methods except increased input, it implies that the particular goods involved are being produced at lower cost or that more units are being produced with the original man-hours and horsepower.

This process has a very direct bearing upon the stability of prices. It might be that the lowering of cost per unit of product would be followed by a corresponding decrease in price. More often, the price stays unchanged and the participants, that is, the workers, management, and owners, receive increased income per unit of labor or capital involved. In such an instance, incomes have increased and prices have not. Essentially, this pictures what is meant by the proposition that when incomes increase at a rate no faster than increases in productivity, no inflation results. Obviously, therefore, how much rising incomes will lead to inflation depends upon their relationship to the rate of improvement in productivity. This chapter will examine these relationships in greater detail.

THE PREREQUISITES FOR GROWTH

It is usually taken for granted that in the present world nations and peoples desire economic growth. Admittedly, other objectives are important as well and the choice between a little more economic growth and, say, a little shorter work week is a difficult if not impossible one to make on any logical basis. However, on any list of economic objectives, economic growth is certain to appear.

Economic growth can be measured in various ways but the most usual definition is the increase of *real gross national product per capita*. This definition recognizes both government and private activity. It associates economic growth with the welfare of the average individual, which is the reason why the words *real* and *per capita* are necessary in the definition. One would not consider an increase in GNP to represent an improvement in the nation's welfare if the increase were entirely fictitious in the sense that no increase in output had occurred. Similarly, even if total output increased, it would not represent an improvement in welfare if the average individual's share decreased, an eventuality that would happen if population increased faster than output. Further, to assure the welfare concept, one must require that the mechanisms of distribution so operate that no segment of the population becomes impoverished. If some gained handsomely while others suffered acute distress, then one could hardly associate an increase even in real GNP per capita with an increase in overall welfare.

It is not necessary to examine in detail the various prerequisites for economic growth. Economists have learned a great deal about the factors that promote and retard growth although their relative importance may change from time to time and from country to country. Four of the more important factors are briefly described below.

(1) The general acceptance of the desirability of economic growth and a willingness to accept and adopt new methods and techniques. Progress involves change and much depends upon whether innovations and the innovator are encouraged or there is popular resistance to change. Governments too can be defensive of the *status quo,* although more and more they are being held responsible for the

economic state of the country, and the widespread commitment to the ideal of full employment makes secular stagnation politically unthinkable.

A further requirement of attitude is a high degree of confidence in the economic and political future of the nation. Consumers continue to purchase television sets on the assumption that power stations will not be destroyed by H-bomb blasts in the near future; businessmen continue to invest and expand productive capacity on the assumption that consumers will continue to have the ability to purchase.

(2) A competent and productive labor force. For some countries this may mean an increase in population, at least where it is as sparse as the United States. The economists who believed in the imminent threat of secular stagnation in the 1930's felt that it would be caused partially by a slowing down or stopping of population growth. The growth of population is favorable to economic growth for two reasons: from the demand side, it increases the number of consumers; from the supply side, it makes more persons available for the labor force.

The size of the labor force depends not only upon the size of the population but upon economic conditions as well, although how the size of the labor force changes in response to changes in economic conditions is not entirely clear. When a recession causes the head of a household to lose his job, his wife and other dependents may enter the labor force in search of a livelihood. Or in prosperity, when a shortage of labor rapidly increases the rate of earnings, some persons who were not willing to work at a lower wage may enter the labor market. However, these are cyclical changes in the labor force and can be disregarded in connection with the growth and inflation problem.

In the long run, there is a strong trend in the United States for the average man-hours worked per member of the total population to decrease. The average American appears to work less and less for more and more. For those who actually work, the hours per week at the job have declined over the years to a present average of about thirty-eight hours per week. Furthermore, with the increase in advanced education, the younger people are delaying more and more the time of entry into the labor force and the older citizens are more likely to retire at an earlier age. Finally, the age composition of the population is gradually changing to include a higher proportion of elderly people who have left the labor force. Against these trends is the fact that a higher proportion of women now work than ever before. The net effect of these trends may be to offset somewhat the contribution of increased population to the labor force, although every individual, whether he works or not, continues to have his full effect on all per capita calculations of GNP or of consumption.

(3) Increased capital investment. Economic growth is closely tied to savings and investment (with allowances made, where necessary, for foreign borrowing or lending). In the manufacturing industry in the United States, capital increased at a more rapid rate than output until 1919, but output has increased more rapidly than capital since 1929. During the whole period, the man-hours–output ratio has fallen steadily, which means that productivity per unit of capital has risen since 1929 while productivity of labor has risen since before 1900.

While the economy as a whole undoubtedly benefits from the investment of capital, individual businessmen will not want to invest and expand their capacity unless their expectations of future profits are favorable. Favorable expectations are created by a high and growing level of consumer (and government) demand for goods and services. From the point of view of growth, it would be desirable to have businessmen maintain a high rate of investment, but if the level of consumption is high, the maintenance of this high rate of investment may be impossible without inflation. This creates the following kind of paradox: If consumption is low or falling, and if therefore businessmen find their sales sluggish, their expectations of future profits will tend to be unfavorable and they may not desire to invest enough to keep the economy at the full-employment level. The national product will then grow at a lower rate than it otherwise might. If, on the other hand, consumption is high, businessmen will be eager to add to plant and equipment but savings may not be sufficient. Desired investment may therefore exceed actual investment, credit may expand, and the result is likely to be inflationary.

In a full-employment situation, consumption and investment are mutually exclusive alternatives in the sense that the economy cannot expand investment without reducing its level of consumption and conversely. To put it in personal terms, if people are too eager to enjoy the comforts of everyday life, they cannot make a large enough provision for expanding the productive potential of the economy. Whatever the forces may be which control savings and investment, they also are a major determinant of the rate of growth of the economy.

(4) Improvement of products and methods of production. By means of improved technology, it is possible to obtain more product from the same quantities of labor and capital. A high degree of research and technical development is required, but no invention can

make a contribution to growth unless it is put to use in business firms. Thus innovation becomes important. Today, major innovation is largely an activity of large enterprises, many of which are no longer specialized producers but pools of management skill and funds of capital which may be engaged in any new venture which promises to be profitable. Also, these large concentrations of capital are particularly suited for undertaking research and development expenditures, and most of the organized research in industry is carried on by large firms in industrial research laboratories. A vast number of lesser innovations represent small improvements here and there in machines or plant design or material handling which generally serve to improve efficiency.

It needs to be noted that the absence of various restrictive practices is also essential for the growth of the economy. One of the dangers associated with the development of large enterprises is, as Schumpeter surmised, the emergence of the desire to "conserve capital." "Conservation of capital" refers to the desire to prevent the appearance of inventions and technological improvements which would tend to make existing capital equipment obsolete. To this should be added the desire to hold markets which have been built up through advertising for particular types of goods. Nevertheless, profits and prestige from innovation appear to be more dominant motives. The overall record seems clearly to show very rapid technological developments, including as a source of cost reduction, improved economic organization of industry.

GROWTH AND INFLATION

One way of considering how inflation may be related to growth is to consider its impact upon the factors which contribute to growth. At first blush, it might appear that there is little relationship between the labor force and inflation. However, if it be true that efforts to check inflation should result in more unemployment than would otherwise be the case, then presumably there would be less total production over a period of years. This would mean not only less consumption per capita but less additions to productive capacity and a lower rate of growth. It is this general line of argument which underlies the criticism of Federal Reserve policy in 1958 for trying to check inflation while unemployment figures were still high.

Again, inflation may seem to be quite unrelated to technical progress. However, there are those who argue that inflation creates an illusion of prosperity and easy profits, and that under such conditions, the urge to improve product or process is weakened. Others argue, with rather more historical support, that expansion and improvement are functions of expanding markets and that the good years, such as 1955 and 1956 (when prices were rising), are the ones in which innovation and expansion occur on a greater scale.

It is not clear how the level of savings and thus the extent of capital formation are affected by high levels of business activity and inflation. The simplest answer would be to say that whenever money incomes rise, savings are likely to rise at an even higher rate. Since the proportion of extra income saved is higher for the high-income groups than for the low-income groups, such a result would be expected whenever there is a shift in income from a low-income group to a higher group. On the other hand, rising prices may discourage saving, at least in certain forms, because saving in the form of assets with fixed value of principal or income implies a loss of future purchasing power for the saver. The latter point is the more relevant the more galloping the inflation is. In the kind of creeping inflation that the United States has experienced over the past two decades, there has been little evidence of a withdrawal from such assets, although some would attribute the stock market boom since 1953 to an effort by many to hedge against inflation. The record for total savings year by year shows no reflection of any such fear, financial savings by individuals being higher in 1957 than in any year since 1945.

When one attempts to find the relationship between inflationary forces and economic growth, historical analysis may be of some value but it is not conclusive. History is made up of such a tangle of forces and interactions that the relationship of particular threads is exceedingly difficult to trace. If one looks at past records, it is not clear that rising prices have encouraged growth, that growth has encouraged rising prices, or that any other combination is regularly recurrent. If one compares the rate of change in income per capita in constant dollars with changes in the price level decade by decade, the record for the United Kingdom shows an apparent inverse reltationship between the two from the seventies to the thirties. The greatest decennial increases in per capita real income came when prices were falling, and lower increases during periods of rising prices. In fact, the decade when per capita real income actually fell (1915–1924 compared with 1905–1914) was the period when prices rose the most. However, the statistical relationship ends with the thirties. Since then, real income in the United Kingdom has risen rapidly and so have prices.

The American statistics do not show as regular a relationship in the earlier years. The peak rate of increase in real GNP per capita was that of the decade 1879–1888 over 1869–1878 when it rose 50.6 per cent and prices fell by 19.5 per cent. However, the decade 1919–1928 showed an increase of 20.9 per cent while prices rose 46.3 per cent. Like the British case, there seems to be a complete break with the earlier pattern in recent years. This may of course be the result of the statistical process whereby the price index is used as a deflator and the result is compared with the price index. Or the apparent relationship in the early years may be the product of some cause affecting both, or even of statistical chance. At least the data do suggest that new factors are at work.

On the basis of the historical evidence, it is difficult to make any generalization about the relationship between price changes and economic growth. The trouble is that the long-term behavior of output and prices is subject to many factors which may quite overshadow any relationship between them. Changes in price level are greatest as the result of wars. During World War I, for example, the war effort caused many types of investment to be neglected for the sake of increasing the output of armaments at the same time that the output of consumer goods was restricted. The government entered the market with a heavy demand of its own for goods and services. The result was that the rate of growth of output declined while the price level rose.

Growth in a sense generates growth because in a generally expanding market each individual firm must expand in order to maintain its share in the market. At the same time, firms must adopt new technology for reasons of survival and prestige, even if profit considerations do not directly dictate such action. On the whole, a high level of business activity tends to press on capacity and encourage expansion. Rising prices themselves act as a business stimulus and contribute to the encouragement of growth. Labor shortages may prompt entrepreneurs to introduce laborsaving machinery and new methods of production and thus increase productivity. In addition, a labor shortage may expand the labor force, as more attractive remuneration, either in the form of overtime or higher wages, persuades individuals formerly not interested in employment to seek jobs or those already employed to work more manhours. The growth process is one of continual readjustment and periods of uneven development may contribute to the structural pressures earlier discussed. But more important is the fact that since growth does involve change and adjustment, it is more likely to correct structural weakness and pressures than a more static situation.

BUSINESS DECISIONS AND PROFITS

One can look at growth either in terms of long-term sweeps of history or in terms of the immediate decisions made by the holders of purchasing power not to consume but to save and by businessmen to make investments. These are the key actions for the expansion or improvement of capacity. In such terms, the performance of prices has somewhat more influence than the record decade by decade seemed to show.

What controls the decision to make an investment? At least, it is clear that one cannot rely upon the simple assumption upon which classical economics was based, that profit maximization is the sole motive. Studies of the process of the making of business decisions have shown that there may be many factors involved. In some instances, the most important factor in investment decisions is the preservation of the business entity, a search for security. This consideration is increasing in significance for two reasons. First is the importance of already established fortunes, so that the holder is no longer greatly concerned with increasing his principal but with conserving it. To these fortunes must be added the flow of savings into funds like pensions and insurance companies, where the obligations are fixed in amount and conservation is the key objective. The second factor is the rise of the managerial class in American business life. The remunerations paid to professional managers are not very responsive to the profitability of the business enterprise but they are extremely dependent upon the maintenance of the enterprise. It is frequently not in the best interest of a professional manager to make a decision which could result in huge profits for the firm at the risk of possible disaster; it is more advantageous to follow a safer course which will insure the continued existence of the firm, even though such a course may not be the most profitable one.

A second basis for investment is the maintenance or improvement of the market position of the firm (as measured in terms of sales). This is one of the surest ways of insuring the survival of the firm. Action designed to keep up with one's competitors may also be undertaken for reasons of pride and prestige. This suggests that the volume of sales may be as much a criterion of success as the level of profit. The maintenance of the market share may necessitate investments which are not dictated by profit calculations.

Still another motivation with reference to investment and expansion has been created by the character of the tax structure. Under present tax laws, wealthier stockholders are frequently better off if earnings are reinvested in the company rather than paid out as dividends. In the first instance, their return takes the form of a capital gain which can be taken in the most favorable year or even avoided, while the dividend pay-out involves an inescapable current income tax charge. Other tax devices, such as special depreciation arrangements, have also been used by the government to encourage investment. Even corporate tax losses may prove to have substantial value. The tax laws might be written to give even more encouragement to investment — the United Kingdom, for example, has no tax on capital gains — but their present bias is clearly in that direction.

Despite the presence of various forms of motivation, it still remains true that the making of profit is of major importance, and that profit in most businessmen's minds is associated with growth. To be sure, the above motivations are not necessarily inimical to economic growth. In fact, they all represent reasons for further investment. However, it is the profit element which is related most closely to rising prices.

The major argument in favor of the hypothesis that inflation promotes economic growth is based on the contention that profit expectations are most favorable in the presence of some degree of inflation. This stems from the fact that the profitability of investment is calculated in terms of money profits. Although it might be more relevant from the overall point of view of the economy to calculate profits in constant dollars, firms operate in current dollars in sales and costs, though they sometimes measure their progress in real terms such as physical volume or number of employees or number of retail outlets. Not only is conventional accounting in terms of current dollars, but it is not easy to see exactly how to correct for price level changes. Furthermore, to the extent that firms finance expansion by incurring debts, certain fixed charges against income exist which are stated in money terms.

There is an undeniable relationship between price changes and profitability. In a demand-pull inflation when wages and other costs are likely to lag behind prices, profits will increase and this will strongly encourage the businessman both by demonstrating the profitability of investment and by increasing the net income available to him to distribute or to reinvest. In a cost-based inflation, prices are likely to follow wages closely as a sort of defensive operation, so that profits will be held at their usual levels. In fact, the price adjustment to offset the wage increase often moves prices up by the same percentage as the increase in wages, which means an actual increase in money profits. Even when inflation does not give positive inducements to further growth, it may keep the profitability of investment on the usual level, thus preventing a disastrous decline in investment and growth. And the growing market contributes to more optimistic expectations.

Some evidence is available on the recent behavior of profits. After World War II, the share of profits as a percentage of total income produced by corporations increased until it reached approximately 26 per cent in 1950 and 1951. Since that time the percentage taken by profits has been generally declining, reaching a point below 20 per cent in 1957. How then does one explain why the declining profit share did not affect investment behavior adversely in 1955–1957? During those years the economy sustained a major investment boom. With expanding GNP, even though the share of profits declined somewhat, the money value of profits was maintained at high levels. The dollar value of corporate profits before taxes declined from $38.3 billion in 1953 to $34.1 billion in 1954, but then increased to $44.9 billion in 1955 and reached a peak of $45.5 billion in 1956. In 1957, profits dropped to $43.4 billion as a result of the recession during the second half of the year. The explanation of these phenomena is the fact that the inflation helped maintain money profits.

Recognizing the various alternative motivations of business firms suggested earlier, it can still be said that the profitability of investment is one important criterion by which investment decisions are made. The evaluation of the profitability of any particular investment depends primarily upon the gap between the profit rate and the interest rate (the going cost of the investment). The magnitude of this gap is relevant because the businessman with funds to invest has to make a choice of whether he wishes to invest his funds in his own enterprise or whether he desires to take advantage of investment opportunities external to the firm, i.e., buy securities of one sort or another. Of course, the relevant profit rate is the rate of net profits after taxes. In order to invest in the firm, the businessman would require a profit rate higher than the interest rate for at least two reasons: investment in securities is a relatively painless way of utilizing funds and requires much less effort on the part of the businessman than enlarging plant and equipment, and investment in securities permits the diversification of the portfolio and thus reduces the risk of investment.

The choice may be illustrated as follows: After a careful study, the businessman estimates that the investment project will earn 20 per cent on the new capital invested. The corporate tax of 52 per cent will reduce this estimated and uncertain return to a little less than 10 per cent. In comparison, he can obtain a riskless, effortless return of 4 per cent on government bonds. If the prospect for gross profit in the enterprise were only 10 per cent, the comparison would be between a 5 per cent net return on the new capacity and 4 per cent in bonds, or perhaps a higher per cent in a more risky security. The decision will turn largely on how the businessman values differences in risk and uncertainty between the two investments.

The level of the interest rate is also often considered to be important as a cost, but in most cases this is an overvalued factor. Suppose that the above project was to be done entirely with borrowed money. If the 20 per cent gross profit was to be earned on 4 per cent money, the net profit after taxes would be about 8 per cent, since the interest cost is fully deductible. If the 4 per cent money were raised to 6 per cent, the net return would drop from 8 to 7 per cent.

While the relative profitability of particular investments may depend upon a comparison between the profit rate and the interest rate, there are several additional reasons why it depends much more on the profit rate itself. In fact, the actual interest rate may be less important to the corporation than its borrowing capacity. Its ability to borrow depends on the general reputation of the corporation, how well its earnings can cover the fixed interest charges required by the prospective issue of bonds and the state of the investment market. If the state of confidence in the economy is favorable, the expectations for profit may be high enough so that the corporation may place its new issue on the market even if the interest rate is high. At some level, the interest rate does become important. No corporation would float a bond issue to yield 10 per cent even if that were the appropriate rate of interest, merely because this is outside the limits to which investors are accustomed. As a matter of fact, the interest rate may even be irrelevant to the investment decision, especially in the case of large firms which frequently do not have to resort to the capital market in order to finance investment projects because their profits are large enough to permit a great deal of internal financing.

PROFIT AND INTEREST RATES

How does inflation affect the net profit rate and the interest rate? It has already been noted that inflation, by raising prices, keeps the profit rate inflated. This is largely true whether one speaks of demand or income claim inflations, particularly if one assumes that the institutional arrangements in the economy of the United States are such that wage increases will occur irrespective of the behavior of prices.

The really important factor from the point of view of the encouragement of investment is the profit rate relative to the investment, not the share of profits in national income. In order to maintain the profit rate, the rate of increase of total profits must be at least as large as the rate of increase in the capital stock. If the percentage increase in profits is smaller, the gap between the profit rate and the interest rate will be narrowed and investment will be discouraged. Inflation can be helpful in maintaining the profit rate, particularly since current profits tend to be inflated whereas existing capital is not revalued at current (higher) prices for the purpose of calculating the current rate of profit on capital.

The inflation and the boom could probably be brought to an end if the rate of interest should rise sufficiently (though this may mean rates considerably above those usually encountered) and lesser increases may have a dampening effect. Professor Irving Fisher of Yale University, for many years the leading analyst in this field, believed that the rate of interest must rise in an inflation because lenders will recognize that the real rate of interest is less than the money rate, and the money rate will have to rise to offset the expected decline in the value of money.

If, however, there is a belief in continuing inflation such as to affect the rate of interest, other forces come into play. When price rises are expected, there is a tendency to change the composition of liquid asset holdings in favor of the variable-price liquid assets, i.e., in favor of stocks, commodities, and foreign exchange in the expectation that they will be most likely to preserve real purchasing power.

The attempt by many individuals to convert cash and bonds into common stocks makes their prices rise and probably rise even more rapidly than the average price level. In turn, this relatively higher valuation of stocks tends to make them less attractive and to arrest the movement into them because it has reduced their yield and created the possibility that they have become overvalued. At the same time, the reduced demand for bonds and the like lowers their price and increases their yield. At some point, the difference between bonds and stocks becomes great enough to stop any further shift.

There are limits to this process of adjustment through liquidity preference. At very low rates of interest, any change in the rate is not going to spur many individuals into action nor will any further increase in the supply of funds be able to drive rates much lower. At very high rates of interest, such money holdings as have not already been attracted into interest-bearing channels will probably not be drawn out by even higher rates of interest. In a hyper-inflation, the price level increases so fast that the relative overvaluation of common stocks creates no fear of possible future falls in the prices of these assets. If the inflation is sufficiently rapid to create the expectation of continued rapid inflation, a flight from cash and bonds into commodities may take place with the result that the interest rate rises even further. This will discourage investment on the one hand and retard the growth of current output on the other by diverting funds and effort into nonproductive speculative activities.

During periods of more moderately rising prices, interest rates have tended to increase, though this does not necessarily mean that one has caused the other. Both are largely the result of the general state of the economy, which, in turn, is in large part a reflection of expectations. The bank rate on business loans increased from 2.10 per cent in 1946 to 4.62 per cent in 1957. The only decline occurred in 1954 and coincided with the only major decline of the rediscount rate. Similar behavior can be observed for bonds of various types: the yield on three- to five-year U.S. government securities changed from 1.16 per cent in 1946 to 3.62 per cent in 1957, the only dip in the gradual rise again occuring in 1954. Increases such as these in the interest rate were only slightly influential in affecting the important profit rate.

The gist of the foregoing arguments is that a slight degree of inflation tends to increase the profit rate and may be beneficial to economic growth. This conclusion must be understood with a certain amount of caution. First, the beneficial effects of inflation on growth, if any, do not necessarily compensate those members of the economy who find their real incomes decreasing or increasing less fast relative to other incomes. Second, if creeping inflation becomes galloping inflation, the probability is that this will be sufficiently disorganizing with respect to the allocation of resources that growth is retarded. Third, profit expectations *may* be sufficiently favorable in the presence of stable prices, particularly if wages do not squeeze profits. And beyond this, the basic argument must be tempered by considerations of the effect of productivity increases on economic growth as well as on inflation.

PRODUCTIVITY AND INFLATION

Figures for growth in the usual dollar terms do not distinguish increases in production from increases in prices. Figures for real growth show total output but do not relate it to the resources and manpower which have been used to achieve it. Productivity is the term used to describe changes in output relative to input. The most usual case is that output increases more rapidly than input. However, productivity may increase without an increase in output, if there is more efficient operation, that is, the use of relatively less labor or capital. Any case of increased productivity would permit an increase in wages and profits without an increase in prices, since the total income available to be paid out would be larger relative to the number of units of labor and capital required.

Recent studies of productivity have calculated it as output per man-hour, as output per unit of tangible capital, and as output per unit of input (which is a combination of labor and capital input). These statistical measures give a total impact measure, lumping together a number of different forces affecting productivity. However, they do eliminate that part of the increase in total output which is the result of simple changes in the quantity of labor or capital employed. Professor Fabricant's study of the long-term record (1889–1957) shows that total physical output of the private domestic economy increased on the average by 3.5 per cent per year, and one-half of the increase could be attributed to the increase in the amount of labor and capital used and the other half to increased productivity.[1] During the last half of the period, total output increased 3.1 per cent, and the increase in resources accounted for one-third and productivity for two-thirds of the gain.

There are difficult problems involved in measuring productivity. Both labor and capital lack a homogeneous standard of measurement. Man-hours, for example, may involve more or less skilled labor. Capital may take the form of machines or buildings or inventory, each with changing characteristics over time.

An illustration of the difficulty in developing measures of productivity relative to labor input was given by the Council of Economic Advisers in the *Report for 1958,* when figures were calculated on the basis of man-hours for which pay is received (plus the hours of unpaid family workers) and also on the basis of man-hours worked (which excludes paid holidays, vacations, and sick-leave). The record on both bases since 1947 is shown in Table I. Since estimates for man-hours paid have increased more rapidly than estimates for man-hours worked, productivity measured on the first basis has tended to advance less rapidly than on the second.

---

[1] Solomon Fabricant, *Basic Facts on Productivity Change,* Occasional Paper 63, National Bureau of Economic Research, Inc. (New York, 1959).

TABLE I — INDEXES OF OUTPUT PER MAN-HOUR, 1947–1957

Year	Based on Man-Hours Paid	Based on Man-Hours Worked
1947	100.0	100.0
1948	104.9	104.2
1949	107.0	105.4
1950	115.6	114.5
1951	118.1	118.8
1952	121.7	123.2
1953	126.2	127.8
1954	129.0	131.5
1955	133.5	136.3
1956	134.6	137.9
1957	137.0	140.9

Source: *Economic Report of the President, 1958*, p. 108.

The increase in productivity per unit of labor is the result of a number of different factors affecting the relationship between output and the quantity of labor employed. One is the development of larger scale production, in which increased output is usually achieved with less labor input per unit of output than in smaller scale production. Larger firms not only tend to have a higher ratio of capital to labor, but a higher capital-output ratio, possibly due to their greater vertical integration. A second is the inevitable and desirable shift from low-wage, low-productivity industries to high-wage, high-productivity industries, whereby the overall composition of the economy is always changing so that, even though no part were improving, the growth in the more efficient industries relative to the less efficient would result in an improvement in the national productivity average. Another important cause is the steady increase in the amount of capital per worker. The labor productivity measure will be little affected if increased output is achieved by an increase in employment but it will be noticeably advanced if it comes from a greater investment in capital. The record seems to suggest that the productivity of labor rose steadily from 1890 to 1929 due to an increase in capital per worker and since 1929 due to innovation which increased the efficient use of capital and thus the efficiency of labor as well.

TABLE II — AGRICULTURAL PRODUCTION ASSETS PER WORKER

	Total Production Assets[1] (Billions of Dollars)	Average Assets per Farm Worker (Dollars)
1940	38.7	3,413
1945	67.7	6,625
1950	95.9	9,625
1955	121.1	14,330
1957	132.1	16,787
1958	140.6	18,381

Source: *Federal Reserve Bulletin* (August 1958), p. 899.

The increase in capital per worker is illustrated most dramatically in Table II, showing capital investment on the farm since 1940. It is largely for this reason that labor productivity in agriculture has risen more rapidly than in most other economic categories. From 1947 to 1957, output per man-hour in agriculture rose 83.8 per cent, in nonagricultural industries 28.6 per cent.

Another factor affecting productivity is the phase of the business cycle for which the record is being made. As an economy approaches capacity operation, further additions of labor are likely to involve hiring less efficient workers or paying overtime. This is also the stage in the cycle when stand-by high-cost machinery is brought into operation. On the other hand, during periods of relative inactivity, while the most efficient labor and capital may be used on the production line, the unit costs may be high because of the fairly fixed contingent of nonproducing workers such as maintenance crews, sales and clerical staffs, and management generally. When output increases, the ratio of producing workers to nonproducing workers also increases, with the result that productivity tends to rise. However, a boom period may lead to considerable carelessness as to the control of costs, and after capacity output is reached, there may be increases in the sales force or the research laboratory without any increase of producing workers. The net effect of these various influences appears to be that labor costs per unit of product fall most rapidly when production is rising in the early stages of the cycle, but are likely to begin to rise in the later stages of an upswing.

Even the cost of materials may enter into productivity perform-

---

[1] Excludes value of dwellings and 40% of value of automobiles. Figures are in current dollars.

ance. In more rapidly growing manufacturing industries, material costs appear to rise faster than labor costs, while the opposite is true in slower growing industries. This may be partly due to the fact that the growing industry undoubtedly has more scope for improving its utilization of labor while it also is pressing upon the less elastic raw materials supply. Other factors also play a part in this picture, but there is some evidence to support the idea that changes in material costs often tend to offset somewhat changes in labor costs.

Finally, there are the increases in productivity which usually are the first to come to mind when the subject is discussed, those resulting from progress in technology and the arts. These may range from the discovery of a new process to a minor improvement on a machine or a better way to arrange the series of operations in a factory. The last several decades have seen tremendous increases in the sums spent by business for research and development, part of which is to develop and improve the product itself and part to make production more efficient. In addition, in this economy of specialization, it often is the machine builder who provides the lower cost process for his customer.

Having this variety of causes in mind, it is probable that inflation itself is not a significant causative factor with respect to changes in productivity, but it may be important to the extent that it contributes to the general state of business. It can be argued that high profits and easy times create complacency and reduce the drive for improved efficiency and more appealing products. While the evidence is not clear, particularly since productivity varies with the degree of utilization of capacity, it would seem more reasonable to expect that improvements can be afforded more easily in prosperous times and are more likely to be done when demand appears to be expanding. The very fact of labor shortage will encourage the increased use of capital as a labor-saving device. While there may be some tendency to cut back on research expenditures during recessions, inventions are probably largely independent of economic conditions but innovation, the exploitation of the invention, may await the favorable moment.

There are clearer lines of causation between productivity and the price level. To be sure, it is not a general pressure on the broad level of prices, but rather a matter of many individual situations. Improvements in productivity per unit of labor are likely to be exceedingly uneven among the different elements in the economy. Thus, using 1939 as a base equal to 100, by 1950 flour and other grain-mill products had lost ground and their index of productivity had fallen to 85.9; anthracite coal had fallen to 87.2. At the same time, labor productivity in the full-fashioned hosiery industry had risen to

162.8 and ice cream manufacturing to 143.4. Agricultural output per worker had increased to 131.0. One bus driver was handling what two had done before although there was little room for improvement in the one driver — one taxicab ratio.

It might be expected that there would be a close relationship between productivity changes and changes in wages in each industry but, in general, specific productivity increases do not contribute much to explain specific wage increases. Observed productivity changes do not tend to equal observed wage changes. Given changes in productivity are accompanied sometimes by small and sometimes by large changes in wages. Unit labor costs, which represent the labor payment per unit of product while productivity represents the man-hours per unit of product, frequently have a tendency to increase faster than productivity: from 1940 to 1947 output per man-hour in mining increased from 102.1 to 114.3 while unit labor costs rose from 97.6 to 180.4; the corresponding figures for the footwear industry (except rubber) are 104.1 to 106.6 for productivity and 99.6 to 193.7 for unit labor costs. Other industries tend to confirm this behavior on the whole. From 1947 to 1957 productivity rose approximately 37 per cent if one includes agriculture and about 28 per cent if one does not. During the same period, average hourly compensation (excluding agriculture) rose about 70 per cent and unit labor costs by about 32 per cent.

Fabricant's study (*op. cit.*) led him to the conclusion that real hourly earnings per hour of work had risen at an average annual rate about equal to the rate of increase in product per man-hour. The long-term trends of earnings in individual industries tended to cluster around the average. He found little systematic difference in rate of increase in hourly earnings between industries in which productivity rose very rapidly and those in which productivity rose slowly; or between those industries with high or low, or relatively rising or falling, ratios of tangible capital to man-hours.

This is not a surprising conclusion. It is important to note that it deals with real earnings and real output. Money earnings may have risen considerably more, but if they did, their increase must have about equaled the rise in the deflator. These figures do not tell whether any added rise in wages caused price increases or the price increases led to successful labor demands. It is fairly clear that labor desires to increase real wages but it negotiates in terms of money wages. There is an inherent momentum in the collective bargaining process that keeps pushing wages upward. Increasing prices and profits stimulate wage increases and these tend to be fairly similar in various industries. After all, there is always the possibility of workers moving from one employment to another, which prevents too wide a gap from developing. It has been found, for example, that in the period 1953–1957, the percentage increase in wages in twelve selected industries was between 18 and 27 per cent. This indicates a much smaller variability in wage increases than in price or profit increases in the same industries which ranged from 3.5 to 31.0 per cent and from 28.9 to 72.5 per cent respectively.

It is at this point that prices enter the picture. It has been pointed out that wages tend to move in a more concerted fashion than either prices or profits. In the case of industries with outstanding increases in productivity and lesser increases in wages, there must be either greatly increased profits or a reduction in prices. In cases with little improvement in productivity and greater increases in wages, there must be either a fall in profits or an increase in prices. If all wages increased at a rate equal to the average of the productivity increases for all industries, then the differences in productivity increase among the industries might be reflected in prices, some rising and some falling, in which case total profits as well as profits for each industry would be unchanged. The average productivity improvement would have gone to labor and the differential rates would have been taken care of by the consumer. This means that prices would rise in industries where the productivity advance was low and vice versa. Given the same assumptions as to wages, another conceivable outcome might be that prices would not change in which case productivity differences would cause equivalent shifts in industry profits. The basic point is that gains through increased productivity as well as failures to gain can be variously reflected among wages, profits, and prices. And there is some reason to believe that the forces at work result in a tendency for prices to rise, a point to be further developed later.

But forgetting the difficult problems of finding the right measures of wages and labor costs, it seems clear that prices will have to rise if wages in general increase faster than productivity in general. Many labor agreements have an automatic increase of 2.5 per cent per year, written into them, based presumably on the estimate that that is their appropriate share of the general increase in productivity throughout the economy. If an industry should have an improvement above the average, it could lower prices or increase profits.

If wages increase by the same percentage as productivity, the relative shares of labor and capital in national income will remain unchanged. If wages increase faster, costs will then be rising and profits will tend to be squeezed. Firms will then be induced to raise prices. Assuming that there exists indeed an inherent momentum in the money illusion which emphasizes the importance of money income, plus the collective bargaining process which tends to propel wages upward irrespective of productivity changes, it becomes important for the economy to achieve large increases in productivity. If productivity increases, economic growth is stimulated and inflation is kept more or less in check.

It should be noted that, when one speaks of wage increases equaling productivity increases, this is usually measured on a percentage basis and implies that other incomes in the industry, such as profits, also increase at the same rate. If a productivity gain was taken entirely by labor, then wage rates would rise more rapidly than productivity and the relative return to capital would fall.

To achieve a balance between productivity and wage increases is certainly not an easy task. To be sure, if productivity increased by more than wages, the profit share would tend to increase, which would undoubtedly bring forth even greater wage demands, thus stimulating wages to catch up with productivity and bringing them into balance. But the increase in wages may exceed productivity, in which case, the ultimate effect is likely to be an increase in prices.

The notion of balancing the two is implicit in the ideal formula given by the Committee for Economic Development (CED), which is that wages should not rise in line with productivity in particular industries or firms, but that wages and profits should both rise at the same rate as the rise of output per man-hour for the economy as a whole (just over 2 per cent a year since 1900 and close to 3 per cent a year since World War II).[2] The same emphasis upon overall balance is suggested in the *Economic Report of the President, 1959* (Washington) in which he repeats the language of the Council of Economic Advisers that "increases in money wages and other compensation not justified by the productivity performance of the economy are inevitably inflationary."

In terms of aggregate economic balance, there is no doubt about the logic that if total incomes vary with total output, prices can be stable. But the economy does not operate by aggregates. Suppose one industry has a productivity increase of 6 per cent and another of zero. Obviously, wages and profits cannot rise in both by 3 per cent, as suggested in the CED formula, unless prices fall in the first instance by 3 per cent and rise by 3 per cent in the second. As a formula for actual

[2] Committee for Economic Development, *Defense Against Inflation* (New York, 1958).

operational use, this implies a statistical measure which is much more certain than those existing at present, the denial of any responsibility to the price mechanism to act as a force for reallocating resources, and a control over wages and prices which would have to be complete. Furthermore, it would freeze the existing ratio in the total economy between wages and profits, since any increase in productivity would have to be distributed between them in the same proportions as existed before in order to have each correspond to "the productivity performance of the economy."

There are important areas in the economy where productivity is not even a usable concept, particularly where services are involved. One wonders how to measure the productivity of doctors or college professors or civil servants. One does know that a doctor with an automobile can care for more patients than one with a horse and buggy, but how compare the productivity of a doctor with penicillin with one without it. These services enter into the cost of living and would have to operate within the formula.

Productivity increases are obviously anti-inflationary, except in the unusual case in which the rapid rise in productivity calls forth an even more rapid rise in wages. If wages fluctuated downward as readily as upward, one might hope that wage increases would tend to equal productivity increases. Wages, however, more and more behave as if there were a definite floor under them. This is not to say that wages have not declined at some times in some industries during the last two decades. The degree of unemployment has some effect on wages and wage increases are more moderate in the presence of unemployment. But in spite of this, the rigidity of wages on the down side is still considerable.

From this one can predict with a degree of assurance that, barring major changes in the institutions of American society, the future trend of wages will continue to be upward. Productivity increases then are a necessary, albeit insufficient, way to check inflation. The reason for the insufficiency of productivity increases is that prices have a certain downward rigidity as well. When wages increase faster than productivity, firms raise their prices to avoid the profit squeeze. When wages rise less fast than productivity, prices are left unchanged on the whole and the difference accrues in the form of additional profits. This factor constitutes an additional ratchet in the wage spiral which has been discussed before. An alteration of pricing and wage setting practices may be as necessary for combating inflation as maintaining steady productivity increases.

ROBERTO DE OLIVEIRA CAMPOS

Two Views on
Inflation in Latin America*

Reference to past experience provides little help in deciding the issue of whether inflationary policies help or hinder the development process in Latin America. Countries such as Argentina and Chile enjoyed periods of substantial growth under inflationary conditions, while Mexico and Venezuela expanded their economies during periods of price stability. Currently, countries which are going through a period of sharp inflation are those which are suffering the most from economic stagnation. This is especially true of those economies which previously prospered under inflation.

De Oliveira Campos ostensibly presents an objective appraisal of the two schools of opinion on inflation in Latin America, the monetarists, who believe that successful development depends on price stability, and the structuralists, who believe that a rise in prices aids development and is a natural consequence of development which should not be suppressed. The reader cannot, however, avoid the impression that the writer favors the monetarist position. He notes that though supply inelasticities and import bottlenecks appear in developing countries, they are often induced by conscious government monetary and fiscal policies. Furthermore, he says, in countries undergoing inflation, the increase in the money supply is much greater than necessary to satisfy normal monetary needs. Thus he is led to the conclusion that the inflation which accompanies development may be considered not as the natural companion of growth but as the result of inflationary policy.

To present the structuralist position objectively, it must be admitted that economic development does create inflationary pressures. Especially in Latin America, which has few easily mobilized idle

---

* From *Latin American Issues*, ed. Alfred O. Hirschman (New York, 1961), pp. 69–79. Reprinted by permission of The Twentieth Century Fund.

factors, increases in investment must be at the expense of a short-run reduction in available consumer goods. Except for a few countries, notably Mexico and Venezuela, the former favored by tourism, the latter by oil exports, balance-of-payments bottlenecks also tend to appear during the period of investment expansion. Thus, granted that during at least the early stages of development shortages occur, the issue between the monetarists and the structuralists actually revolves around the question of whether these shortages should occasion monetary and fiscal controls to stabilize prices or whether they should be allowed to produce their natural market consequences, higher prices.

The monetarists, of course, favor the former policy, while the structuralists favor a passive response, or inflation. While de Oliveira Campos is certainly correct in emphasizing that the inflation can be controlled, he does not credit the structuralists with sufficient reasons for advocating inflation. The disadvantages of severe inflation—disrupted demand and supply conditions, sharp alterations in real income distribution, political instability, and balance-of-payments problems —are obvious; but sophisticated structuralists believe in orderly, even predictable price rises. Moreover, they see economic advantages to inflation not noted in de Oliveira Campos' paper. When prices rise, they argue, interest rates fall in a real, if not money, sense. In addition, profits rise, and workers, deluded by a Keynesian "money illusion" are satisfied with higher money wages even if these wage increases do not match the price increases. On the external economic front, structuralists admit that inflation leads to import bottlenecks but consider that exchange rate restrictions and import rationing are small prices to pay for the economic stimulus of inflation.

Politically, monetarists usually favor internationalism, internal stability, expanded foreign trade, and, if possible, foreign aid. The structuralists are usually nationalists who tolerate internal turmoil and see the development process as one confined to the country's own efforts and resources, with little recourse to foreign (United States) "intervention." There is something paradoxical in the structuralist position in that a strongly capitalistic economic view of development —with low real interest rates, high profit, and low real wages inducing growth in private investment—is often linked with an anti-capitalistic political philosophy.

Unfortunately, the most recent Latin American economic experiences cannot provide support for either school, mainly because the pace of economic growth has slackened throughout the area. A rough estimate yields a figure of from 1 per cent to 2 per cent for the current average annual rate of growth in per capita real income. With this sluggish growth rate, which is not only the average but also the typical rate for all but a few countries, the monetarist-structuralist argument is presently academic. Some countries are undergoing inflation, especially Argentina, Brazil, and Chile (coincidentally the countries which have had the greatest past growth). Other countries are stabilizing prices by following the monetarist policies of monetary and fiscal controls. None is now enjoying significant growth. Perhaps price activity, whether neutral or inflationary, has little relevance to the growth process.

IN several Latin American countries now facing problems of acute inflation, there is a sharp theoretical and policy clash between two groups which, for want of better terms, I shall call the "monetarists" and the "structuralists."

To the "monetarists," views are ascribed that are close to those imputed to the International Monetary Fund, even though several of them dissent from the IMF in many respects. The "structuralists," on the other hand, claim to have support for their views in the studies of the Economic Commission of Latin America, even though official ECLA reports do not show the fatalistic view of the inflationary process in Latin America nor the degree of scepticism toward monetary and fiscal policies that is implied in the "structuralist" view.

In a heroic oversimplification, the views of the two contending schools of thought — at least as expressed in Brazil — can be summarized as follows:

The "monetarists" hold that:

(a) Inflation has ceased to promote development and in fact has become incompatible with it; even those countries that managed to have inflation and development are now facing an acceleration of inflation and a deceleration of development;

(b) Inflation must be stopped quickly, before it degenerates into explosive tensions, and the only effective method seems to be the curbing of excess demand through a prudent combination of monetary and fiscal policies supplemented by international financial assistance;

(c) Most of the alleged supply inelasticities and bottlenecks are not autonomous or structural, but are caused by price and exchange rate distortions generated during the course of the inflationary process itself.

The "structuralists," on the other hand, hold that:

(a) Inflation is a natural accompaniment of growth;

(b) Inflation cannot be curbed through monetary and fiscal means without provoking unemployment or stagnation of growth because of supply rigidities;

(c) The instability of export proceeds, generating a capacity-to-import bottleneck as well as supply inelasticities inherent in the growth process, renders it impossible to curb inflation in the short run; it in fact renders desirable a *gradual* attack on inflation, except to the extent that foreign assistance becomes available to render the supply of imports more elastic.

To a certain extent the two contending views are less different than they might seem, the divergences being more of method and emphasis than of substance. There is, however, a *hard core* of dispute which centers mainly on the usefulness of monetary and fiscal policy as well as on the relationship between structural factors and the inflationary process itself.

NOTES ON THE "STRUCTURALIST" VIEW

An implicit assumption of the "structuralist" view is that a sharp distinction exists between the inflationary behavior and policies of less developed countries taken *as a group,* on the one side, and the developed countries as a group, on the other; and accordingly a separate theory is needed to account for such discrepant behavior.

This approach, as noted recently by Arthur Marget, tends to overestimate differences *between* the two groups and slur differences *within* the groups. For instance, *within* the less developed group Brazil followed expansionist monetary policies and is suffering from acute inflation. Mexico pursued more prudent monetary and fiscal policies and has had only a moderate rate of inflation. *Within* the industrialized group, France, until the recent stabilization program, followed inflationary monetary policies while Germany adhered to a conservative approach. It may be said, in this respect, that there is (or was until recently) a greater similarity of behavior between Brazil and France than between Brazil and Mexico.

In short, countries in similar stages of development and achieving comparable rates of growth had varying degrees of inflation and varying monetary experiences, depending on the set of monetary and fiscal policies they chose to adopt.

Is a new or modified theory of inflation, emphasizing supply inelasticities or bottleneck factors which are judged to be inadequately covered by the "demand-pull" or "cost-push" theory, in fact needed for the understanding of inflation in Latin America? Is there room for a "structural" theory of inflation, which would regard changes in money supply as merely passive adjustments to irresistible autonomous pressures generated by bottlenecks in the import capacity, or inelastic food supplies or institutional arrangements?

On the ground of the data and comments I have seen, this effort at theorizing would seem an exercise in "unnecessary" originality; but I am of course open to persuasion.

To naïve and unsophisticated minds like my own, a number of questions would occur immediately: Why not undertake a statistical effort to detect such correlation as may exist for different countries in Latin America, between (A) expansion of the effective money supply,[1] indicating a passive behavior of the monetary authorities, (B) rate of price inflation, (C) rate of growth in real product?

A few things would undoubtedly stand out.

(a) In the heavily inflated countries the rate of expansion in the money supply has been of such an order of magnitude (20 to 30 per cent per year) as to outstrip any realistic possibility of growth of the supply (via increases in the real domestic product plus net imports); at that rate of monetary expansion no economy, even though highly developed and presumably exempted from major inelasticity or supply bottlenecks, would fail to have inflation.

(b) No clear relationship appears to exist (if anything the correlation is negative) between the rate of inflation and the rate of development. The highly inflated countries (Argentina, Chile, Bolivia) tended to stagnate; some of the low-inflation countries (Mexico, Venezuela, El Salvador, Ecuador) seem to be developing fast. For the others there is a mixed picture but it may be said tentatively that (1) where inflation coincided with rapid development, the latter can best be explained by other factors (absorption of foreign resources, improvement in the terms of trade) than by the full utilization of capacity supposedly brought about by inflation, (2) in recent periods

---

[1] Supply of money corrected by changes in velocity; strictly speaking the relevant concept would be that of "changes in liquidity," involving not only money but also "near-money." But (a) near-money is less important in Latin America because of incipient financial markets, (b) data are not usually available on money market assets.

the acceleration of inflation has coincided with a deceleration of development.

(c) The above data would give a *first hint* that the behavior of inflation in Latin America would seem to conform pretty much to what might be expected in the light of old-fashioned theories.

It might of course be argued that the above investigation would merely represent a *tautological* illustration of the inflationary process. The relevant question then would be: Why is it that the monetary authorities in Latin America find it so peculiarly difficult to behave actively and usually confine themselves to register on the liability side (money supply) all of the asset creation plans of the government sector, private sectors and net foreign balance? Several answers might suggest themselves:

(1) *Those pressures are irresistible in the process of growth.* This answer would *prima facie* be unsatisfactory as (a) some of the Latin American countries achieved high rates of growth without inflation or with moderate inflation, (b) even the overinflated countries (Brazil, Argentina) have achieved, in discontinuous periods of their history, rapid growth with nothing like their present inflation, (c) given demand pressures for governmental or private investment in development programs, it does not follow that the money supply must be passively adjusted to ratify those programs; after all, investment programs can be financed by taxes, by foreign loans, by physical rationing of consumption, by shifts in the composition of investment, etc.

(2) *Supply inelasticities, institutional rigidities and the capacity-to-import bottleneck (pressures from the real or income side) are the active factors and monetary expansion a residual.* This line of argument would encounter the same difficulties mentioned above, namely, (a) some countries managed at times to control inflation despite bottlenecks and (b) there is no intrinsic organic reason why bottlenecks and inelasticities should be greater in Brazil and Argentina, for instance, than in Mexico or Ecuador. Again it is very difficult to resort to bottlenecks and inelasticities to explain the Argentine inflation at the beginning of the Peronist era.

The upshot of this initial statistical effort would be to bring out clearly, to my mind, that the role of old-fashioned monetary and fiscal policy is vitally important. Money factors are not residual but at the very core of the process. The inflated countries are those that choose incompatible targets.

The Role of Inelasticities and Bottlenecks

It is an underlying assumption of the "structuralist" school that such inelasticities are (a) peculiarly inherent to the growth process in Latin America, (b) autonomous and causal factors of inflation.

A visitor to ECLA in Santiago cannot help feeling that the thinking of the "structuralist" school has been affected by the peculiarities of the Chilean inflation and fell into the trap of generalizing this experience. Chile has had, I am told, almost 95 years of fairly continuous inflation; the attempts to fight it were until recently half-hearted efforts to conceal an open inflation by converting it into a *repressed inflation,* which created still more distortions than the open one. In the course of the process, price or exchange rate distortions discouraged investment in certain sectors (food production, transportation, power, exports) and bottlenecks arose; these bottlenecks now appear to have caused the inflation when they actually resulted from it. It is true that, once generated, bottlenecks may begin to play an independent causal role; and they certainly render the fight against inflation more difficult. In this sense the original *variables* have been converted into *data* of the problem; but this does not invalidate the basic distinction between *natural* bottlenecks and *induced* ones.

Structural bottlenecks indeed come to one's mind when discussing the Chilean inflation; somehow they seem much less relevant when one discusses the Mexican or Venezuelan situation. And for the Argentine inflation, only a fertile imagination would attribute a causal role to bottlenecks and food supply inelasticities; they were the result of Peronist policies (pegging of rates of public utilities and transportation, taxation of agricultural exports to subsidize industrialization, etc.) and not the causal factor of the Argentine inflation, even though they now complicate tremendously the problem of combating it.

We all recognize of course that there are *leads* and *lags* in the development process; balanced growth, *stricto sensu,* is almost a practical impossibility. But it does not mean that these need to become cumulative and self-feeding; this only happens when policies are pursued that convert self-correcting disequilibria inherent in the growth process into induced and cumulative ones.

A *model* explaining one of the possible methods of bottleneck generation could thus easily be constructed in the following fashion:

(1) Excess demand arising from the pressures in the foreign sector (wartime export surpluses not offset by unspent export taxes or by imports) led to price inflation.

(2) Attempts were made to repress inflation not by curbing general excess demand but by controlling certain key prices (basic foodstuffs, rail transport, electricity, interest rates).

(3) Private voluntary savings and investment were discouraged and replaced, after a time lag, by deficit-financed government investment.

(4) Inflation was aggravated, bottlenecks arose and "structural rigidities" were created.

On the basis of the Latin American experience it may be quite possible to demonstrate that, to a large extent, the alleged bottlenecks were originally inflation-induced, even though at a later stage they may become inflation-feeding.

(a) *Bottlenecks in transport and electricity.* In most Latin American countries (Argentina, Brazil in particular) utility rates have been congealed, or the capital base for rate determination frozen at the "historical" cost, despite rising costs. Results: (a) stoppage of investment, (b) net disinvestment, (c) bottlenecks.

(b) *Food supply.* Rather than curbing general excess demand it seems infinitely easier for governments to establish price control of basic foodstuffs leading to the following results:

— in the case of food for internal consumption:

(i) subsidization of demand for consumption, thus aggravating the price pressure;

(ii) reduction in the relative profitability (as compared with industry or the import trade, for instance) of the food production sector and consequently disincentive for investment in agriculture;

(iii) diversion of land from productive to unproductive uses.

— in the case of agricultural production for export:

(i) emergence of repressed inflation through overvalued *exchange rates* that tax export production;

(ii) manipulation of internal producers' prices by state export monopolies that tax the export sector in order to subsidize industry.

(c) *Rigidity of the savings function.* Freezing of interest rates to decrease costs for investors acts as a tax not on spenders but on savers; in many cases, legal interest rates become negative, forcing would-be savers to de-monetize their savings by investing in real estate or in foreign currency, or else to run the risk of irregular financial transactions to achieve a positive interest rate.

(d) *Import capacity bottleneck.* A prolonged inflation is obviously a powerful generator of "capacity-to-import" bottleneck. In Latin America the countries that suffer acutely from such bottlenecks are precisely those that have indulged in multiple-rate practices. And this of course is not a mere accident of fate, for various reasons.

(i) There are usually sibsidized rates for certain basic or so-called "rigid" imports that are held to be important cost-of-living items (fuel, wheat) as well as for machinery and equipment for essential projects. The net result is that wasteful consumption is encouraged, there is a perverse substitution (against the competing national product or substitute product), investment demand is overstimulated by the artificial reduction of the private cost to the entrepreneur, but often with an increase in social costs to the economy as a whole.

(ii) Subsidized import rates go hand in hand with pegged rates for certain exports which thereby become subject to heavy taxation; this results in a disincentive to expansion and diversification of exports. There are of course cases when exports taxes are advisable and necessary (to create stabilization funds, to correct domestic overproduction, etc.) and the multiple-rate mechanism may be a convenient and flexible technique for taxing exports. But clearly many of the Latin American countries have abused multiple-rate practices and come dangerously close to killing the hen that laid the golden eggs. (Argentina is a case in point.)

The purpose of these notes is not to deny that once supply inelasticities have been created through a long process of inflation (1) they may begin to exert a derived causal role, (2) they make the combat against inflation more difficult and painful than it need otherwise be, (3) stabilization programs may have to adjust themselves to the fact that in its initial phases the repressed inflation may have to be converted into an open one (prices in the controlled sectors being allowed to rise in order to correct previous bottleneck-creating price distortions), (4) the combat against inflation would require monetary and fiscal policies in a broad sense, including programs for a more productive reorientation of public and private investment, as well as a foreign aid component.

A Note on the Capacity-to-Import Bottleneck

It is often somewhat uncritically assumed that a limited capacity to import is an independent datum of the inflationary process in Latin America. Even though this may be true in the very short run it is important to determine to what extent it is again an "induced" bottleneck arising from deliberate policies that combined internal inflation with external overvaluation, and aimed at financing the rise of import substitution through export taxes, rather than through general taxation and other incentives; or from the lack of foresight in building up reserves in boom periods to avoid excessive import contradictions in loan periods.

Practically all of the inflated Latin American countries biased their development program in an anti-export direction. That is most certainly the case in Brazil and Argentina; Chile also discouraged for a long time the expansion of copper investments, and through multiple rates, which have the effect of export taxes, discouraged diversification of exports.

Mexico and Venezuela did not indulge in development policies biased against exports and did not experience the same acute import capacity bottlenecks. Nor can the problem be assumed away simply by saying that Mexico had naturally elastic exports in the form of tourism and Venezuela enjoyed the oil and iron ore bonanza. The fact is that Venezuela might have adopted policies that would hinder investment in oil and minerals, as Brazil (in the case of minerals and oil) and Argentina (in the case of oil) managed to do rather effectively, and Mexico might not have cashed in on Brazilian and U. S. mistakes on coffee and cotton.

But even when the effect of inadequate export policies is discounted, it may well be that there is a residual bottleneck in the capacity to import. This is in fact likely to be the case whenever exports cease to be (and there is no reason why they should always be) the leading "growth" sector of the economy. In other words, it is quite conceivable that exports may tend to grow at less than the required rate, despite the adoption of rational development programs. This may be because of long-run downward terms of trade, lower income and/or price elasticities of demand for primary products, etc. (e.g., Prebisch's thesis, which may have validity in the case of certain countries and products because of the combined effect of Engels' law, technological savings in raw materials, synthetic substitutes, or an ambivalent behavior of mining concerns as exporters of raw materials in less developed countries and consumers in developed countries, etc.).

This situation in fact was envisaged in good old classical international trade theory. This "natural" as opposed to an "induced" lag in the rate of export growth as compared to the overall rate of development is indeed implicit in Cairne's time-honored theory about the stages through which a developing country's balance of payments is likely to pass. Young debtor countries are supposed to have an import surplus covered by loans; as they mature the inflow of loans is offset by debt payments; finally, they become capital exporters and develop an export surplus.

Upon those who emphasize the limitations of the capacity to import as an "original" and almost unavoidable bottleneck explaining a good part of the irresistibility of inflationary "real" pressures in

Latin America rests the burden of proving that this bottleneck has not gone beyond the normally expected gap, precisely as a result of inflationary policies and anti-export-biased development programs. The severe constriction of the import capacity in Brazil and Argentina, for instance, seems to have been engineered by (a) excessive export taxation through exchange rate or price distortions, (b) misguided import substitution policy, (c) the wrong method of financing import substitution.

On the Active or Passive Behavior of the Monetary Authorities

There seems to prevail among the "structuralists," alongside an underestimation of monetary policies, a much too narrow concept of what is meant by monetary and fiscal policy.

Clearly, given pressures emerging from public expenditures, volume of investment and export volume, the monetary authorities need not act passively but may react in a number of ways. Given, for instance, an autonomous wage increase of political origin, the monetary authority may choose to allow credit expansion by a margin considerably smaller than the cost push. In this case it will force the entrepreneur to absorb part of the cost increase, through reduction in profits, to liquidate inventories, and/or to increase productivity. Nor can it be assured that the fatal result of such measures will be unemployment and reduction in the level of real investment in industry. If the entrepreneur considers the governmental policy to be firm and irreversible he may not choose to contract employment or investment in the industry but will rather monetize real assets (real estate, buildings, etc.), liquidate "near-money" assets, or reduce personal consumption. If of course the monetary authority starts from the fatalistic assumption that the cost-push pressures cannot be resisted without unemployment or reduction in real investment, then there is no "monetary" cure for inflation. But then there is no "real," "structural" or "institutional" cure either. For the basic contradiction of the "structuralist" view seems to be that precisely because the "structuralists" emphasize the sluggishness of supply in less developed countries and the import limitations, they ought to conclude logically that the only possible effective attack on inflation would be a contraction of excess demand; precisely what the "monetarists" have advocated all along.

The research on bottlenecks is of course extremely useful for fiscal and monetary policy to play an even more useful active role; and that is the line of reconciliation between "monetarists" and "structuralists." For a lot can be done by fiscal and monetary weapons to correct bottlenecks without additional investment that would merely aggravate excess demand; this can be done simply through the alteration of price incentives and reorientation of government investment from less productive to the bottleneck sectors (shift from military expenditures to investment in agriculture). Nor can it be assumed, as many "structuralists" assume, that a reduction of the over-all investment level in the course of stabilization programs is detrimental to growth. In the first place, this reduction may be purely temporary, soon reversed by an upsurge in investment. In the second place, a better composition of investment may emerge (with the reduction of speculative investment) with a consequent improvement in the capital-output ratio, so that a lower overall volume of investment may be compatible with an acceleration of real growth.

It remains to be seen whether this will in fact be the result of some of the stabilization programs now attempted in Latin America (Argentina and Colombia, for instance). In my view there is a fair chance that this will occur.

SUMMARY

Out of the confusion of argument and counterargument regarding the causes and effects of inflation, the following tentative conclusions can be reached. Unfortunately, for the student who seeks unequivocal answers to these questions, many of the following conclusions are somewhat indefinite.

1. Inflationary periods of the post-war era have been confined to three distinct periods—the immediate post World War II years, the Korean War years, and the period of creeping inflation of 1955–1958. The inflations associated with the wars were the more severe by far.

It is impossible to state definitely whether demand-pull or cost-push elements were more important as causes. Even for the postwar period, when consumer demand was obviously expanding, it is not certain that wage and profit pushes were not strong contributors to the inflationary pressures.

2. Examining the two types of inflation themselves, and their variants of demand-shift and mark-up inflations, one finds that a cost-push inflation is much more difficult to control than the demand-pull type. The latter requires the application of restrictive monetary and fiscal practices to drain off excessive demand. The former is not susceptible to direct controls. What is needed is restraint on the part of labor and management in their wage and price policies. Since most of the cost push is attributed to wage demands, formulas for responsible wage policies have been suggested.

3. The most widely discussed noninflationary wage formula is the one that limits individual industry, or firm, wage gains to the percentage increase in national productivity. In addition to the many criticisms of this formula, all related to the fact that its application interferes with market action, there is even some argument that the formula is inherently inflationary, given the assumption that the country (government) is pledged to a full-employment policy. While the employment effects may be negative for the individual firm that tries to take its productivity gain in the form of higher factor returns, taking the economy as a whole, a general gain in productivity may be translated into constant prices with higher factor income, or lower prices with constant money incomes. The latter result is deflationary,

but the former is not inflationary. In either case, general productivity gains permit economic growth and improvement in average standards of living.

4. There is some question as to whether the effects of inflation are harmful, as most writers suggest, or beneficial to an economy. While all admit that sharp inflations disrupt the productive process, there are many who argue that moderate price rises stimulate investment and growth. Inflation raises current profit rates relative to interest rates, but investment decisions are based upon expectations, and it is debatable whether current experience is a strong enough factor to outweigh the more definite elements that influence the businessman's decision to invest; inflation does not necessarily widen the gap between expected future gross profits and costs.

5. The role of inflation in the development process has been argued without definite agreement on the consequences of inflation. Among Latin American economists, "monetarists" support a policy of price stability, and "structuralists" argue for freedom from controls designed to limit price rises. The evidence is not conclusive in support of either position. In fact, it is even debatable whether price behavior plays a significant part in development's progress.

SUGGESTIONS FOR READING

An exhaustive study of the important aspects of inflation was made by Martin Bronfenbrenner and Franklyn D. Holzman, "Survey of Inflation Theory," *American Economic Review*, LIII (September 1963). The article also contains a comprehensive bibliography on the subject. Besides the Ackley paper presented, many other writings with different viewpoints on the causes and cures of inflation appear in *The Relationship of Prices to Economic Stability and Growth*. A general view of inflation, with emphasis on its monetary aspects, is presented in a collection of papers, *Inflation: Causes and Cures*, compiled by Thomas O. Waage (New York, 1949).

Relevant to cost-push inflation, many writers have considered unionism inherently inflationary because of unions' insatiable wage demands. Important expositions of this view are made by Henry Simons, *Economic Policy for a Free Society* (Chicago, 1948), and Charles E. Lindblom, *Unions and Capitalism* (New Haven, 1949). For a contrasting view, see John T. Dunlop, "Wage-Price Relations at High Level Employment," *American Economic Review, Papers and Proceedings*, XXXVII (May 1947). Conflicting views on the cost push inherent in unionism can be found in *Impact of the Union*, ed. David McCord Wright (New York, 1951), and in *The Public Stake in Union Power*, ed. Philip Bradley (Charlottesville, 1959).

Although the period of the creeping inflation is usually considered the most significant evidence in support of the cost-push theory, Richard Selden, "Cost-Push vs. Demand-Pull Inflation," *Journal of Political Economy*, LXVII (February 1959), notes that during 1955–1957, the industries with the greatest price rises were those with the strongest demand. In another attack on the cost-push position for the same period, Lowell E. Gallaway, "The Wage-Push Inflation Thesis, 1950–1957," *American Economic Review*, XLVIII (December 1958), argues that the inflationary fiscal policy of the period was independent of any attempt to offset unemployment induced by a wage push and that consequently fiscal policy and practices rather than cost push were responsible for the inflation. A frequently cited statistical study of the relationship between inflation and unemployment is A. W. Phillips, "The Relation Between Unemployment and the Rate of Change of Money Wage Rates in the United Kingdom, 1861–1957," *Economica*, XXV (November 1958).

A general study of the wage-productivity issue appears in the collection *Wages, Prices, Profits, and Productivity*, The American Assembly (New York, 1959). For an earlier presentation of the formula of the Wage Guidepost see *Defense Against Inflation*, Committee for Economic Development (New York, 1958).

On the theoretical dispute about the effects of inflation on Latin American development, other papers in *Latin American Issues* besides the De Oliveira Campos essay presented are David Felix, "An Alternative View of the 'Monetarist-Structuralist' Controversy," and Joseph Grunwald, "The 'Structuralist' School on Price Stability and Development: The Chilean Case." For the Spanish reader, Barry N. Siegel, *Inflación y Desarrollo, Las Experiencias de México* (Mexico, 1960), describes the Mexican experience in pursuing the monetarist policy of relative price stability during development. For the dispute in other areas see *Inflation*, ed. D. C. Hague, International Economic Association (New York, 1962).